The Mystery of the Tuscan Hills

A Travel Guide in Search of the Ancient Etruscans

Morris M. Weiss, M.D.

Bloomington, IN   authorHOUSE   Milton Keynes, UK

AuthorHouse™
1663 Liberty Drive, Suite 200
Bloomington, IN 47403
www.authorhouse.com
Phone: 1-800-839-8640

AuthorHouse™ UK Ltd.
500 Avebury Boulevard
Central Milton Keynes, MK9 2BE
www.authorhouse.co.uk
Phone: 08001974150

© 2006 Morris M. Weiss, M.D.. All rights reserved.

No part of this book may be reproduced, stored in a retrieval system, or transmitted by any means without the written permission of the author.

First published by AuthorHouse 12/28/2006

ISBN: 978-1-4259-3061-5 (sc)
ISBN: 978-1-4259-3060-8 (hc)

Printed in the United States of America
Bloomington, Indiana

This book is printed on acid-free paper.

Dedication

To Professor Albert Leonard Jr., who took a chance on me.

And to my wife, Terry, who has steered me safely through the byways of Etruria and life.

Contents

Dedication		v
Foreword		xiii
1	**The Core**	1
	A. Introduction	1
	B. The House	6
	C. Chuisi	8
	D. Montepulciano	11
2	**The Thermae of Etruria**	15
	A. Saturnia	19
	B. Emperor Augustus Takes a Cure	21
	C. Le Thermae Montecatini	22
	D. Casciano Thermae	23
	E. San Casciano dei Bagini	24
	F. Chianciano Thermae	24
3	**The North**	26
	A. Florence and Environs	26
4	**The Northwest**	35
	A. San Gimignano	35
	B. Pisa	35
	C. Volterra	36
5	**North Central**	39
	A. Siena	39
	B. Tenuta di Spannocchia and La Piana	42
	C. Murlo	46
	D. Monte Oliveto Maggiora Monastery	47
	E. Grosetto/Rusellae	48

6	**The Northeast**	51
	A. Arezzo	51
	B. Cortona	54
	C. Perugia	54
	D. Lake Trasimeno (Lago Trasimeno) & Environs	56
7	**The West Coast**	57
	A. Cerveteri	58
	B. Pyrgi	60
	C. Tarquinia	61
	D. Vetulonia	64
	E. Populonia	65
8	**Central**	67
	A. Lake Bolsena	67
	B. Orvieto	70
9	**The South**	73
	A. Etruscan Rome	73
10	**Return to the Core—Finale**	80
	A. Sarteano	80
	B. Cetona/Monte Cetona	82
	C. Radicofani	83
	D. Mount Amiata	84
11	**Etruscans Outside Etruria**	86
	Appendix	101
	Bibliography	103
	Index	105

Foreword

The cool air touched my face as I stepped down into the Etruscan tomb carved into the living tufa. It was a hot, dry Tuscan July day, and the noon sun scorched the earth above as I entered the world I had been looking for. All I had read, studied, excavated, and visited over the past twenty years came in a great rush of images, and I knew I was finally ready to assimilate the culture of this enigmatic people of which we know so much—but in reality, so very little.

The great painted tombs of Volterra are masterpieces of art and tell us much of Etruscan lifestyle, philosophy, and religious beliefs. These tombs are crowded with tourists, so the painted walls are protected by Plexiglas and the chambers are air-conditioned—to try to preserve their beauty from the bacteria and body heat of tourists. In contrast, and more to my liking, the austere, cruder tombs of Chuisi, and the precise architectural city of the dead at Orvieto—usually free of sightseers—allow the imagination to soar.

This monograph will encompass a series of portraits, or snapshots, of the Etruscans—as I perceive them. It will not be an encyclopedia of Etruscan sites and cultural history, nor a travel book of Tuscany. The bookshelves are filled with elaborate coffee-table tomes of the flowers, birds, villas, and museums in Tuscany. And traditional travel guides in many languages abound, most repeating the same information. What I have tried to reveal is a Tuscany that most travelers drive through or around, and view from a distance—but rarely "see." At the risk of sounding pretentious, and after several trips to Tuscany, learning to understand the Etruscans seemed the best way to get my hands around this exquisite space—truly one of earth's Edens.

After all, they were one of the earliest societies with the technology to harness their environment and create a garden to live in.

I begin with considerable trepidation and humility. After all, other writers with large followings and reputations have given their best to put down on paper Tuscany's effect on their psyche.

George Dennis, the English savant, produced in 1878 the first complete travel book on the Etruscan civilization. His was the original, and to this day the best, description of Etruscan monuments and art. No writer—either traveler or academic—has come close to his nineteenth century accomplishment. Dennis is the Gibbons of the Etruscans, if you will.

Mark Twain wrote of his travels in Italy in *The Innocents Abroad*. Twain's is a totally irreverent survey of Italy, as he crosses the grain of the country from north to south. He seems to hate Italy, and especially his guides, whom he carps never stop talking.

He likes the trains and roadways more than the art, of which he confesses he knows little and does not want to understand or care to see. My read of his Italian sojourn: Twain is an American snob and the original nineteenth century ugly American.

He understands the Mississippi River culture, but was in a canoe without the proverbial paddle on his Huck Finn raft in Italy.

D. H. Lawrence's view of Etruscan places in his travelogue, *D. H. Lawrence in Italy,* was an artistic tour de force: a rapid-fire stream of consciousness his creative, neurotic mind conjured up during a brief few days of touring Etruscan tombs and monuments, with incredible insights and with his brilliant use of language.

The other American, William Dean Howells, whose Etruscan journal *Roman Holiday* was a gift to me from my son John, is a generic travel account. I suspect he dressed every day in coat, tie, and top hat as he toured Italy at the turn of the twentieth century. Accurate he is, but too dry and humorless a writing style for my taste.

The composition and layout of this book required a decision. Should I produce a feature movie of Tuscany, starring the Etruscans, or a photo album and portrait gallery? Vignettes won the day.

Scientific history, as understood by modern historians, requires precise information, so we are left with a series of battles, plagues, and dry events—no matter how skilled the writer. The good painting reveals the inner self of the subject as interpreted by the artist on the canvas. The biographer is more the painter than the scientific historian. His job is to try to get into the mind of his subject—to understand why he acted as he did. The Greek writer Plutarch, in his *Lives*, understood this perfectly; that's why his works survive over two millennia. Plutarch drew portraits of his subjects.

Using this frame of reference, I will present selected Etruscan sites, arbitrarily chosen by myself—not simply because they were important places in Etruscan history, but because to me they presented an opportunity to look into the Etruscan mind. I want to better understand this amazing people, whose language we cannot read, because the Romans and barbarians destroyed all that they wrote, except for several thousand gravestone inscriptions and a few other scraps of religious ritual. Oh, if we could only have Claudius's twenty-volume history of the Etruscans. Very probably the last copy went up in flames with the great library in Alexandria. It seems unlikely that even fragments remain hidden behind the wall of an anonymous scriptorium in an ancient monastery in Italy, France or Ireland—hidden from view because the history was penned by a pagan Roman emperor.

1

The Core

A. Introduction

Who were the Etruscans? When discussing them, we always use the past tense. But the present tense is also appropriate, because if you walk along the streets and marketplaces of today's hill towns and observe the faces of contemporary Tuscans, they strongly resemble the visages on the tomb paintings and the ceramic sculpted figures on sarcophagi lids. The genetic remnants remain and are different from the classic equine Roman nose. Yes, the Romans, over several centuries, slowly wiped out Etruscan political identity. However, the art of divination, religious rituals, public health projects (draining malaria swamps), love of gracious living, medical knowledge, and metalworking are just a few of the Etruscan contributions to Roman civilization that continue to influence Western thought to this day.

Slowly, over the past one hundred years, archaeologists and art historians have teased out the Etruscan legacy. For two thousand years, the Romans have been credited with advances for which they owed a large debt, having simply expropriated these from the Etruscans.

Since the Etruscans were a different people than the Romans, what are their primeval roots? Scholars have been discussing and arguing about this for twenty-four hundred years. Herodotus, the Greek historian, writing in the mid-fifth century B.C., some three hundred years after an established Etruscan civilization can be clearly recognized in the archaeological record, states they came from Lydia (modern western Turkey) in the thirteenth century B.C. At this time, Lydia was suffering a great plague and King Atys sent his son Tyrrhenus, with one half of the population, to establish a colony on the west coast of Italy—hence, the Tyrrhenian Sea. Along this stretch of Italian coast, between the Tiber River to the south and the Arno to the north, were the original Etruscan city states. The Greeks living in colonies south of the Tiber, about modern-day Naples, call them Tyrrenoi. Modern Tuscany is a corruption of Tusci or Etrusci—the Roman name for the Etruscans, who it is believed called themselves Rasna or Rasenna. The reason for this dichotomy, I do not understand.

Anyway, the plot thickens. In the first century B.C., the great Greek philosopher Dionysius of Halicarnassus declared emphatically that the Etruscans were indigenous people in Italy. These two opinions reigned until the eighteenth century A.D., when the scholar Nicolas Freret tried to prove they came to Italy during the Indo-European migratory waves from northern Europe to the Mediterranean in the early second millennium B.C. But enough of this speculation. Currently, experts say the Etruscans were always there in one form or another, and are descendants of the late Bronze Age/early Iron Age Villanovan society.

Although many Etruscan religious symbols and other hints suggest an eastern Mediterranean origin (to which I am attracted), the reality is that people must always have lived and enjoyed the rich land, temperate climate, hot springs, and abundant food and wines we now call Tuscany. I suspect the word was out even in prehistoric times: save your Euros, get a thatched and mud hut villa in Tuscany, and enjoy your final years under the Tuscan sun—and soak your aching joints in the ubiquitous hot springs (thermae).

Just a few words on the Etruscan skills and personality, as you trundle about the hills and valleys of central Italy. This information has helped me appreciate what I have purposely sought out, and what I simply stumbled upon.

The family was very important in Etruscan society. We see this in their tombs, where several generations of wealthy merchants and royal families are ensconced. The tombs are carved into the soft tufa and resemble their domestic architecture. The tomb walls are covered with scenes of family dining and funerary banquets, dancing, musicians, acrobats, hunting, swimming and diving sports, just to name a few of the myriad events that filled their lives.

Tuscan wives enjoyed equal status with their husbands—even in the grave. The famous sarcophagi that abound in the museums show husband and wife reclining together for eternity. The bottoms of the sarcophagi were mass-produced in workshops, but for the wealthy, the reclining figures are portraits of the deceased—commissioned before their deaths. Although the Romans copied much of Etruscan mores, they certainly did not give their wives as prominent a role. The husband was *pater familiaris* ("father of the family") and his word was law. The women in the family, along with the slaves and children, had subservient status. The Etruscans, it is clear, had very close family ties.

The mountains of Tuscany contain much iron and copper, and the Etruscans were accomplished metal sculptors, as well as potters and fresco painters.

They also were accomplished engineers, who built roads and hydraulic projects that drained the swamps around Rome and then the Maremma to alleviate malaria—a deadly curse in this part of the world, even into the time of Mussolini in the 1930s and '40s. Most of the Etruscan tunnels that drained the swamps had filled over the centuries and had been long forgotten, until they were recently rediscovered.

Motive

What prompted this most recent intrepid adventure, and why this site? First of all, this was to be my seventieth birthday trip, and the longest sustained vacation of my life—just over four weeks. Second, Abbazia di Speneto is in the center of ancient Etruria and the home of the Etruscan civilization, an object of my curiosity for more than twenty years.

Archaeology is my avocation and my passion. I have trundled about many classical excavations as a grunt, including two seasons at La Piana (near Siena), a small Etruscan settlement away from the large city-states—the usual site of major digs. La Piana is just about thirty miles from Abbazia di Speneto.

In the twenty years between digging at La Piana and this trip, my wife and I and friends made several other excursions to Italy.

One sojourn involved visiting the hot-spring spas, or "thermae," used by the Etruscans, Romans, and the peoples of Italy, up to today. Even before the Etruscans—who spanned the ninth to the third century B.C.—it is very likely the Neanderthal and the Neolithic peoples of 30,000 B.C. to fourth millennium B.C. used these hot springs that have bubbled to the surface for tens of thousands of years.

This trip allowed daily excursions to many of the major Etruscan sites in central Tuscany, the core area of the scattered Etruscan confederation of twelve major city-states, extending from Rome on the Tiber River in the south, to Florence on the Arno River in the north. To the east are the Apennines—the spinal column of Italy—and to the west, the Tyrrhenian Sea, that portion of the Mediterranean that lies along the western coast of modern-day Tuscany.

This trip was twenty years of planning in my mind and two years to find the right site to live, and from which to explore. In the process, we included adventurous friends, not afraid to get hot and sweaty during the day, and to enjoy wine, olives, and cheese in the evening while discoursing and debriefing on the day's discoveries.

Our goal was to find the Etruscans, try to better understand this advanced society, and, in the process, perhaps to better understand ourselves. For me, as a physician, I have long known science alone is not enough. To totally understand a patient, the doctor must know not just the science, but also the cultural influences that affect the way the patient views you, his physician, and his society. This helps us determine the way we face and handle the vicissitudes of illness. To acquire this wisdom, we must study the seminal civilizations that have contributed to our contemporary society. The Etruscans are one such group and, even though we cannot read their language, there is much to learn that could help me become a better healer.

Preliminary History and Thoughts

Who are the Etruscans? I briefly alluded to when and where in the Italian peninsula this enigmatic people flourished. However, to better understand what motivated us (my wife, Terry Weiss, M.D., our teenage son David, and assorted friends and family) to take this study trip and be able to savor the best of Tuscan food, wine, scenery, and archaeology sites, a primer of Etruscan cultural history is in order. First, let me offer a skeletal look at the Etruscans, and then fill in the skin, muscle, nerves, and a few vital organs. Then, as we proceed about the highways and byways of Etruria and explore the Etruscan countryside, the reader hopefully will be better able to identify with and enjoy the exhilarating experience of exploring and probing an Etruscan site.

Beginning

Our rental car steadily climbed a gravel road, through a series of switchbacks, to our summer farm house a few hundred meters above the paved valley road. I thought of an earlier trip of switchbacks, taken to get to the heights of Macchu-Picchu in Peru, as well as the donkey ride into and out of the Grand Canyon. This site, our summer home, was known to us only by a photo image. How would the family react to this setting?

Our first trip up this rutted, gravelly road—at times resembling a goat pathway more than a roadway—was a challenge for our car. To constantly change gears, in our underpowered, stick-shift, midsize Renault sedan made me think of *The Little Engine That Could*. I looked out the rearview mirror at the contrail of whitish-gray dust we created. Our car was superbly designed for the autostradas at speeds of 140 to 180 km per hour, but was rebelling against this hostile terrain and an amateur rural driver. The tires are designed to push water from under themselves, so those amazing velocities achieved on Italian highways are a bit safer. With no water to push laterally, the tires scratched and clawed and scattered the small stones randomly, making gripping the road difficult at best.

This five kilometer ride from the valley to our farmhouse soon became routine. My shifting improved—not ever perfect—and the poor, dusty car and ill-conceived tires lasted the month we inhabited our five hundred-year-old farmhouse on the property at Abbazia di Speneto. We accomplished the month's driving without a stalled engine, a vapor lock, or a flat tire. However, the poor car's skin looked much like the dermal covering of a coal miner with a lifetime of coal dust that can never be completely scrubbed off.

In the Middle Ages, the 2,500 acres of farm land supported this abbey of moderate size. Scattered throughout the farm are seven other modernized farm houses, all nestled in the hillsides and none visible from any other. The abbey is a modern conference center, with the church now restored, and is used for small business and professional meetings. The conference attendees, of course, stay in the farm houses—not a bad way to learn and plan.

B. The House

The house was perfectly sited—on sloping land near the summit of an Etruscan hill. The last few yards of the road up to the house puts you at an elevation near the level of roof eaves when you park the car. A few stone stairs lead down to the entrance. You soon pass into a small atrium—simply decorated with a round oaken table and a seventeenth century armoire used for storing dishes. The next room is a large dining area, with a huge, perfectly square table, seating sixteen (four on each side). An open kitchen and living room with a large fireplace are just off the eating space. Two bedrooms are off the living room. On the second floor are four more bedrooms, two of which open to the backyard of the house, since it is built on a slope.

The building is of fieldstones, with walls three feet thick. The roof is of sienna clay tiles, which are ubiquitous to this part of Italy. The tiles are overlapping and rounded, of course. Each slab of clay, when still wet and malleable, is bent over the thigh of the tile-maker. This produces a tile with a large curve and a smaller curve, in the shape of the ceramicist's thigh. When they are fired, the result is roof tiles that nicely overlap and fit snugly together. This method of production remains unchanged from Etruscan times, dating to at least the ninth century B.C. The peasant house on the abbey estate originally stabled the farm animals on the first floor and the family on the second floor. This half-millenium-old rustic farmhouse is now completely modernized, with a bathroom for every bedroom and armoires for storing clothing. There are no closets in Italy.

The spectacular view from the house varies dramatically with the time of day. The land is tilled on three sides of the house, with the fields beginning a few yards away. Behind the house, at the crest of the hill, is the wooded home of deer, lynx, fox, and giant hares—just to mention a few. The July–August season is dry and only stubble of wheat remains in the fields. Down in the valley, wild boars feed along with the deer in the evening, when the temperature cools and the shadows appear. The boar and his mate, with the piglets in line behind mother, is a memorable sight. Across the valley are more towns, draping over the tops of the hills like a scarf that fits the contours of your shoulders, or an ice cream cone beginning to melt.

The most conspicuous landmark seen from LaBusterna (the name of our home) is Radicofani, a hill town with a castle and tower, with Monte Amita—the highest peak in Tuscany—in the distance. The road to the house teems with avian wildlife. Coveys of quail and grouse are constantly dashing across the road, but are agile enough to never get hit by your car.

Behind the house is a modest concrete box called a swimming pool, rural Italian style, with a few chaises set in an open space, free of trees and brush, and the perfect spot to sip wine, relax, and debrief from the day's adventures in the surrounding hilltop towns. I must not forget the grape arbor adjacent to the pool, a quiet haven of shade to read and update your journal, usually with a soft evening breeze. At night, the deer and other creatures use the pool as a source of water during the summer drought.

The night sky is beyond redemption. At this time of year, clouds are almost non-existent. The firmament reveals billions of stars, easily seen with the naked eye. My pocket star guide that I remembered to slip into my suitcase allowed instant recognition of summer constellations. Even though I had lain on my back on previous archeology trips in Sicily, Egypt, Crete, and Tuscany, never did the sky seem so well defined. The Milky Way truly looked like milk—real milk, not the skim or 2 percent we drink in America now, but the milk of my youth, delivered daily to our side door with a layer of yellow cream and, when shaken, a rich white liquid with real body. Well, this is what the Milky Way resembled over our house, as I lay on a chaise beside the pool.

C. Chuisi (Roman: Clusium; Etruscan: Clevins)

If the traveler wishes a portrait of rural Tuscany and a true Etruscan experience, Chuisi is a must on your itinerary map. This is the quintessential hilltop town where Neolithic, Etruscan, Roman, and medieval civilizations are gathered in a small, unspoiled space.

Chuisi was one of the twelve cities of the major Etruscan (dodecapolis) federation, with her greatest influence from the seventh to the fifth centuries B.C.

Chuisi lies on the main north-south road from Rome to the principal cities of Tuscany and those north of the Arno, and it was surely the major artery of travel even in prehistoric times. Travelers, traders, and armies for millennia passed through Chuisi. Fortunately for the modern traveler, Chuisi has been bypassed by the autostradas (primarily A1), and is left to age gracefully like the patina on an ancient ceramic garden vase. During the Dark and early Middle Ages, fifth to tenth centuries A.D., malaria in the marshes of the Valdichiana contributed to her decline, from which she never fully recovered.

Geography, as always, controls most of human building decisions, and the hilltop where the ancient town is nestled is high enough that the train station is only about halfway up the hill. So, when you approach Chuisi from the valley, just a short distance from the A1 exit, an eyesore of an American-like strip mall appears with a new Italian concept—the Supermercato with the appropriate name of "Etrusche." Bear right and follow the road on a modest ascent. About halfway up is a wide junction; if you continue to bear to the right, be ready for modern Chuisi, home to modest-income families. The area of the train station and bus depot is surrounded by small streets filled with shops selling the necessities of daily living.

To the locals' credit, they maintain the system of specialty shops for food, clothing, furniture, hardware, and appliances, and have resisted the Wal-Mart concept. The first chink in this armor is occurring with the Etrusche Supermercato in the small shopping center, with music, shoe, and jewelry shops, near the A1 exit.

Unless you are in need of a train schedule or car repair, keep moving up the hill and soon the road opens onto the main piazza.

Inside the piazza, which is no more than one or two acres, is the cathedral, surrounded by small trees, and park benches inhabited by gnarled retired men, idly gossiping, smoking, and taking in all the activities slowly moving about them. This is a late medieval town and the houses have been repaired and rebuilt countless times. Fortunately, modern architecture, which would look so out of place, is nowhere to be found.

Finding a place to park is easy down one of the side streets; then meander the few yards back up the hill and just stand a few moments to watch the rhythm and dance of this public space. Activity appears to be in slow motion to Americans, but it's the normal cadence for Chuicians. For a moment, I did not want to invade their space. But a fresh lemonade stand in the shade of the trees next to the cathedral dragged me across the street and into their mini-universe, as I sought to quench my noontime thirst on a hot, breezeless, humidity-free, sunny Tuscan day. The small streets that come off the compass corners of the piazza are worth exploring.

Our summer house was reasonably close, so whenever we visited Chuisi, we'd stop at the small family-owned businesses—always in the first floor of the building. There were separate shops for daily bread and meats, pastries, vegetables, and the cheese and pasta groceries, which made picking up what you need (and suddenly find you cannot live without) an adventure in living, and not a gruesome grocery shopping chore.

By the time our month was over, we nodded to the old men on the park benches and were greeted by the merchants.

Chuisi offers much more. The regional Etruscan museum is the best in all Italy. I say this without reservation, since I dragged my family through most of the regional museums, from Rome to Florence. The two great Etruscan museums, the Villa Guilia in Rome and the wing of the National Museum of Archaeology in Florence, must be visited by anyone interested in the Etruscans.

My favorite is the Villa Guilia, a papal summer house on the Tiber, where the Pope went on a hot summer afternoon or evening to rest in the most beautiful Roman-style nyphaeum I've ever seen—and which I greatly enjoyed myself. And, besides, there is a reconstructed Etruscan temple on the grounds. The Etruscans used stone foundations and ceramic tiles and decorations on the roof, but the walls and columns were of wood, so nothing of original Etruscan structures survive, except piles of roof tiles resting on a limestone foundation. This structure allows your senses to imagine what their temples must have looked like.

The two museums I mentioned are filled with room after room, and glass case after glass case, of Etruscan treasures, but the museum in Chuisi has it all in a smaller space—beautifully displayed with one or two important items from each Etruscan century, and without the overwhelming effect of the bigger museums. The analogy is of a small family grocer with one or two jellies and mustards, instead of shelves with thirty or forty different kinds of jellies and a dozen mustards that one is bombarded with in the megastores of today.

The Chuisi museum (Museo Civico Archeologico, also known as the Museo Nazionale Etrusco) is in a beautiful neoclassical building directly across the perimeter piazza street from the cathedral (duomo)—built originally in the sixth century A.D. and rebuilt in the eleventh century.

What you need to be aware of is that directly underneath your feet in this area is a network of catacombs, quarried from the fufa and limestone by the Etruscans, Romans, and other inhabitants of this city. Much of this is open to the public by guided tours, in well-lit spaces, with adequate safeguards to prevent falls and bruises. Above the greater part of the catacombs, the cathedral sits in an area laced with ancient Etruscan and Roman walls, all well marked and offering a comprehensive appreciation of the use of public space.

The visitor soon realizes how much has transpired over the past 2,500 years—and in reality, how little has changed. The underground tour is capped off by an easy climb to the top of the campanile, a bell tower, adjacent to the duomo. This, like many bell towers, was originally for military purposes. At the top is a 360-degree panoramic view of the valley below. Today, fields of cornflowers, sunflowers, and vineyards fill your vision—but in times of war, no one could get close to the base of the Chuisi hill undetected.

If you are into Etruscan tombs, go back to the museum and book a tour of the Etruscan fifth century B.C. tombs found scattered about the base of the hill. Over the centuries, many have been found and looted, but enough have survived to fill the museum collection. For a very modest sum, the museum curator will drive you to several well-preserved tombs, or you may follow in your own vacation-mobile.

I recommend the Tomb of the Monkeys (Tomba della Sciamma), Tomb of the Lion (Tomba del Leone), and Tomb of the Grand Duke (Tomba del Grandduc). The tombs are not as sumptuous as the famous painted tombs of Volterra. But you will have the tombs to enjoy by yourself, without the pressure of throngs of tourists pressing from behind and blocking your view in the front. From these tombs, you can get an idea of Etruscan domestic architecture, since some are carved to resemble their homes. (That way, the deceased will feel "at ease" in the afterlife.)

I will end my Chuisi portrait with an afterthought. On summer Saturdays, around the cathedral, there is a flea market. On old card tables, the items for sale—surely recycled many times over the past hundred years—are an assortment of rusty farm implements, bent kitchen utensils, old military insignias, and a few vintage postcards, as well as some nice ceramic pieces.

I picked up a few additions to a small collection of postcards showing ancient sites that is slowly accumulating in my library.

D. Montepulciano

Montepulciano is a dignified, but slightly scruffy, hilltop town with a population of approximately 14,000. The apex of Montepulciano is 665 meters above sea level with a view of southeast Tuscany and Umbria. Montepulciano is famous for several prominent Renaissance personalities, including Angelo Ambrogini (1454–94), the tutor of Lorenzo de'Medici.

The area is famous for wines, including Brunello, that many say is the finest wine in all of Italy, and the equally famous Vino Nobile di Montepulciano.

Make your own choice; you cannot go wrong.

Montepulciano is accessible on the Siena to Viterbo and Rome Road. Leave Siena by the Porta Romano. If you enter the city at the Porta al Prato, follow Via Roma to Via Cavour, and look for Palazzo Bucelli (#73). With Etruscan and Roman artifacts and various inscriptions embedded at eye level in the façade of the Palazzo—pieces of urns and sarcophagi dominate the wall. These were collected by the owner, an amateur antiquarian. Here are scraps of Etruscan writing representing people's names carved in tomb mantles, then removed to be embedded along with his other artifacts. This brief encounter allows the casual walker a chance to see Etruscan lettering, if you are not familiar with other sources.

Keep climbing the very steep Via Roma until you emerge at the top of the hill at the rebuilt medieval fort that walled off part of the city. The fort wall leads you to the Piazza Grande and, of course, the town's duomo. Have a good look around and catch your breath after the climb! Negotiating Montepulciano is a lesson on how to navigate Etruscan hill towns.

The natives, of course, have legs like steel bands and know no other lifestyle. Even the most gnarled old grandmothers (known as Nonnas) patiently plod up the steep streets with the day's cheese, bread, and fruit in the ubiquitous plastic bag on one wrist and often a small dog on a leash in the other hand. They tend to lean forward into the slope of the hill at an angle not unlike The Leaning Tower of Pisa. Like The Tower, they seem perfectly balanced.

As for myself, with my two titanium hip replacements, this technique I practiced, but admittedly never perfected.

Make your way back down the streets—this time, leaning slightly backward whenever the pitch increases. Just outside Montepulciano is the Tempio di SanBiago. This magnificent church is a must for everyone visiting this region. Do not miss it! On any given day, tourists will visit so many churches they eventually blend into one another. Test yourself the day after a full morning and afternoon of touring and try to recount the details of the six or eight houses of worship you were in that day. The Tempio di SanBiago will be a visit you will always remember.

You approach Montepulciano on the road to Pienza. The turnoff is onto a cypress-lined lane of beauty and tranquility that sets you up for the church that suddenly appears on your left. The trees stop, and the church sits on a level field surrounded by a low retaining wall. The building is a masterpiece of High Renaissance architecture and the piece de resistance of the architect Antonio Da Sanguello il Vecchio. The structure was erected between 1518 and 1534. This is truly one of the greatest structures of this period. When I came upon the church, I had the impression that a giant helicopter must have set the church down in this site. There are no major trees directly surrounding the building. She simply stands there in haughty splendor. From a distance, the masonry gives the viewer a picture of massive strength, but when you get near the subtle lines, the massiveness gives way and a more humanistic feeling envelops you.

The quiet surrounding the building follows the visitor inside. Again the proportions do not overwhelm, but give the feeling, at least for me, of St. Peter's and the duomos in Florence and Milan. This church is lightly visited compared to the big city cathedrals, so moments of reflection or prayer are possible, surrounded only by the stillness of the church, not several hundred worshipers. I particularly enjoyed sitting on the surrounding masonry wall and enjoyed the bucolic countryside spreading out in the valley at the foot of Montepulciano.

My recommendation is to finish your visit in the early evening, with dinner to follow at La Grotta, the restaurant just across the road from the Tempio di SanBiago. Our two most memorable dining experiences occurred at La Grotta. The first dinner with friends and family was inside at a long table, immaculately set up with pink linen and spotless, sparkling wine glasses, in a room with a high vaulted ceiling. The staff is warm and friendly, and patiently explains the specialty dishes to newcomers like ourselves. They expect to serve you over a three- or four-hour period and help you choose the proper wine for each course.

The wine for the entree will be Vino Nobile di Montepulciano—the local vintage of international renown—truly a gift from the

Gods! The pastas are all homemade. I would recommend taglioni con carciofi i rigatoni (thin noodles with artichoke and bacon). There are many other entrée choices, but La Grotta is noted for pork in pecorino and truffle sauce (filetto di maiali in salso di pecorino e tartufo).

Personally, I did not think we could repeat a second session as divine as the first, but two weeks later we returned. (Included in our group was the restaurant critic for our city newspaper in America.) This was an early August evening with temperature in the low 70s with a light breeze, and we ate outside under a large grape arbor with surrounding cypress trees, sipping wine and talking of endless reminiscences from seven o'clock.until just before midnight. Our sommelier was a delightful 20-ish Tuscan beauty whose face resembled the women on Etruscan tomb and vase paintings that have come down to us.

As we exited the restaurant, the magnificent Tempio di SanBiago was bathed in a near full moon. We climbed into our cars and carefully (and I mean *carefully* because of the wine we had consumed) wound our way through the gently curving back roads of Tuscany to our hilltop house. If you are ever in the area, dine at La Grotta. We will always remember those two evenings.

2

The Thermae of Etruria

The thermae (hot water spas) of Etruria are vital to understanding the native culture of this area. Guide books rarely emphasize how important and fundamental they are to the fabric of Tuscan life. These hot water baths have, of course, been bubbling to the surface since geological times. The water in a majority of the springs is warm or hot when it reaches ground level, but this section is limited to natural hot springs, which are discussed—and their virtues extolled—in the earliest historical records. (The subject of hot baths, and the water warmed by hypoclausts [furnaces] developed and refined by the Romans, is another story.)

The Roman writer Pliny and his contemporaries write of very advanced Etruscan knowledge of hydrotherapy, herbs, plants, and animal products useful for the treatment of medical conditions. The Romans observed and learned from the Etruscan herbalists. They surely were clever and proficient pharmacologists. We do not know if the Etruscans had professional physicians and druggists, or if they, as the Romans after them, left treatment of the family, slaves and farm animals to the head of the household (*pater familiaris*).

I will discuss in the section about Florence the research of Charles Godfrey Leland ("the Forgotten American"), who clearly established the tradition of Etruscan pharmacology and medical care in rural Italy from the sixth century B.C. to the twentieth century A.D.

I believe the Roman system of family and veterinary medicine was inherited from the Etruscans. Early Romans were farmers, as were the Etruscans, so the same system seems plausible. An analogous system of medicine is in the medical encyclopedias found in every rural and urban American home in the nineteenth and early twentieth centuries.

The medicinal use of the plants and animals that surround us surely was mixed with the use of the hot springs scattered throughout Etruria. After a lifetime of climbing up and down the hills of Tuscany, and performing the manual labor of this pre-industrial society, most people had some form of arthritis rather early in life. If you were fortunate to survive into your sixth, seventh and eighth decades of life, I suspect nearly everyone availed themselves of the soothing effect of hot water baths, with various mineral content, regardless of social and economic status.

Today in Tuscany, therapeutic bathing and hydrotherapy is available for every pocketbook.

We also must remember that the Etruscans had an amazing knowledge of human anatomy. Tens of thousands of small votive statues have been found in caches at the site of sanctuaries dedicated to healing gods and goddesses. The small figures—the vast majority made of terra cotta (fired clay)—show in accurate detail which part of the supplicant's anatomy was causing the pain: torsos with a cutaway view of the heart and lungs; abdomens with cutaway views of the liver; gall bladders and colons; penises; uteri; eyes; feet; and fingers were just some of the organs accurately depicted.

This combined knowledge clearly means the Etruscans were skilled at what we would call internal medicine, pharmacology, physical medicine, and probably some types of surgical procedures. I believe it is safe to postulate that the Etruscans developed this knowledge themselves, because the Roman writers honestly admit that most of what they know about these medical subjects came from the Etruscans—and most importantly, they trust this knowledge more than what Greek doctors brought to Rome. Greek medicine came to Rome in the Hellenistic period (third to first centuries B.C.), but Greek doctors as a rule were not trusted by the average Roman citizen and *pater familiaris*.

So this Etruscan indigenous, naturopathic, holistic medicine, mixed with superstition, curses, and prayers, to this day is a thread woven into the Tuscan fabric of daily living.

On one of my digs in Tuscany, we were living near the farmhouses of the peasants who took care of the farm and villa where we were housed. The matriarchal strega (witch), who was stated to have the ability to talk "chicken," was the first consulted when a child or one of the peasant farmers became ill. If she was unsuccessful, they then went to the priest. And finally, the third person consulted was the village doctor. Again, this triad of medical care pointed out by Charles Godfrey Leland exists to this day.

The medical history of waters and spas in Tuscany is documented over the past twenty-four hundred years. Roman writers in the centuries before and after Christ's birth mentioned the medicinal springs frequented by the Etruscans. The story of water for drinking and medical therapy has, in the past two decades, been tackled by historians of continental Europe and Great Britain, and the literature is now enormous. But we will concentrate on the natural springs. Before Rome built cities with large populations, water was obtained from wells and cisterns. Hot springs were simple pools and holding tanks for a few people to enjoy.

What we want to know is: where in Tuscany are the sites used by the Etruscans? As we will see, many are still in active use and, as they are repaired and enlarged in modern times, Etruscan buildings are turning up. A new collaboration with developers and archeologists is slowly developing so that the origins of these natural hot springs can be investigated.

In the last few years, Etruscan ruins are being found on a regular basis.

Thermae

In Greater Italy (the Italian peninsula and Sicily), there are more than 150 natural thermal stations. As early as 1960, more than a million people each year received fifteen million treatments at Italian spas. I do not have recent data, but the numbers and enthusiasm for hydrotherapy have continued to grow, and facilities have expanded and been modernized.

In Tuscany, Montecatini is the queen of all the facilities and I will discuss her and a few others, but it seems appropriate to mention a few sites famous in antiquity and surely used by the Etruscans.

The adventurous traveler can enjoy looking for and scoping out these sites, all of which are off the beaten path:

- The Bath of Caldana (Aquae Populonia), near Campligia Marittina. Pliny called this the "Bath of Vetolunia."
- The Baths of Vicarello, on the shores of Lake Bracciano. Also called the Baths of Stigliano.
- Cerveterii (Caera) Spas.
- Taro Spas (Baths of Verrata), near Civitavecchia, near Lake Bracciano.
- The Baths of Volterra, south of the city, near San Felicae Gate.
- The Sulphur Baths of Saturnia, which we will discuss in depth below.
- The Baths of San Casciano (Fontes Clusini) near Cuisi—probably the modern baths of Thermae Chianciano.
- The Baths of Vignone—a small thermal station near Lake Bolsena.
- Bagno Vignoni, which still has a hot bath in the local hotel. The original bath is closed.
- The Bagno San Fillipo—the world's smallest spa, near San Querco d' Orcia, near the Bagno Vignoni (see above).

The Baths of Serapis (Bagni della Serapi) is an open air, sulfurous spring in an open, overgrown field at the junction of two country roads. This site is easy to miss and difficult to find on these byways. I would never have found the place if it were not for my wife ("The Navigator"). She has an unerring compass and global positioning device encased in her calvarium, and has always—and I mean always—guided us to the obscure sites we often search for, with nary a wrong turn.

In a former life, Terry must have been a homing pigeon—or better yet, a monarch butterfly.

The Bagni della Serapi is located near La Lettghetta (the warming pan)—a site known as the Waters of Passeris—noted by the Roman writer Martial and recorded on the famous Pleutinger Map. This site also is identified with the hot springs near Bacucco—described by the poet Dante as the "Bulicame." We walked about this site, waist-deep in dry grass and weeds. A small circular pond contains the hot, sulphurous water rising from the earth, and follows a course in a narrow trough into a shallow pool, where bathers gather.

A narrow footpath from the paved road leads to the pond where bathers—who ride bicycles, motor scooters, and the tiny cinquecento Fiats—lie partially submerged in the warm water. Hidden in the grass and weeds, and protruding from the hard-packed earth, are small piles of Roman bricks, using the opus reticularis construction method. This site is ideal for further archaeologic investigation. I am certain Etruscan building foundations will be found, since in the vicinity, carved into the exposed tufa, are numerous Etruscan tombs in very deteriorated condition. This site, we can say, is the most primitive of the hot springs and primarily frequented by locals and tired travelers.

A. Saturnia

Saturnia is another open-air hot spring that produces enough hot water to create a rapidly flowing stream. Saturnia is almost due west of Lake Bolsena, but a bit north. Saturnia is an adventure worth undertaking if you have a bathing suit in the car and are driving north from Rome along the coastal road to Cerveteri, Civitavecchio, and Tarquinia—all Etruscan towns. This area is rich in Etruscan lore and culture, and wherever you turn, our Etruscan friends have left their mark.

Saturnia suddenly appears as you drive along a narrow rural road. The site is marked, but it's still best to look carefully. You soon find yourself in a gravel parking area, filled with cars, motorcycles, and all types of campers. There is a small restaurant and refreshment area, and prices are very reasonable. Make your way along the path and follow the parade of families, wending their way to the waters. The small rapid stream where you park suddenly widens in a series of cascading falls (only 12 inches or so high) that invite you to wade in (only a few inches deep).

Over the ages, the water has created small pools, about the size of your derriere. Sit down in one and lean against the falls, and just let the warm mineral waters massage you. The rocks are slippery from the sulphur and sulphur-loving algae that coat them.

I carefully made my way into the stream and then stayed put, because I was worried about slipping and dislocating my titanium hips. But my companions frolicked in the falls which end in about 250 yards, in a shallow, wide pool filled with rocks.

Then the water runs off into a narrow stream and disappears into the countryside.

License plates from all over Europe are found in the parking area. Everyone is courteous and relaxed. The water produces wondrous relaxation, and friends and family enjoy the entire experience in a gaggle of languages. Saturnia is worth the diversion from the main road and the usual guidebook attractions.

You can almost see the Etruscans of two millennia ago bathing beside you, soothing their aching bones and joints.

Pitigliano

Pitigliano is just east of Saturnia. There are no major Etruscan excavations, but it is worth a drive-by from the road. The town sits atop a two-tufa outcropping, with many rock-cut tombs of Etruscan and Roman origin—easily viewed from the road below. Pull over to the shoulder, take a look and perhaps wonder, as I did, how they were able to cut these tombs into the virtually vertical rock face.

I remember seeing in China the most extreme example of man's ingenuity before power tools. I was seated on a narrow, bamboo raft that was slowly pulled through a shallow river with one thousand-foot cliffs on both sides, i.e., a river gorge. About five hundred feet above the water line were several small, cave-like tombs carved into the rock. Later, in a regional archaeology museum, I was shown the hollowed log sarcophagus with the desiccated mummy inside found in these tombs in recent times. The estimated age is one thousand years.

One wonders how many slaves it took to dig the tufa tombs in Italy below Pitigliano, and how many fell to their death or suffered serious orthopedic injury. Pitigliano has an interesting history because here in the seventeenth century A.D., a ghetto was built by Jews fleeing religious persecution. Other towns nearby that are worth a peek (if time allows) are Sovana and Sorano.

In this area, the true flavor of Etruscan life in Tuscany can be felt. There are rolling hills and fertile valleys with abundant water and soil capable of producing verdant fields of grain, and slopes filled with grapes and olives. We must not forget the wildflowers that speckle the roadside in every nook and cranny with delicate and colorful petals.

B. Emperor Augustus Takes a Cure

Before discussing a few of the modern indoor warm and tepid water spas, a few words are in order about the medicinal property of cold or "icy" water baths. Professor David Soren of the University of Arizona has been excavating since 1995 near the Etruscan city of Chuisi. Close by Chuisi are the towns of Chianciano and Mezzomiglio, where Professor Soren has collaborated with Italian archaeologists and historians, and is systematically exploring the Etruscan and Roman ruins lying under and adjacent to the modern facility. He is finding evidence of Etruscan architecture under Roman and contemporary buildings.

Slowly, we are learning about the hydrotherapy as employed by the ancients, and this adds to our understanding of ancient medicine as a discipline in its own right. It also helps twenty-first century physicians understand the cultural aspects of our profession—a theme that I keep referring back to. This idea motivates my travel and my home study almost on a daily basis. It is the obligation of every physician to study and apply scientific peer review journals and evidence-based medicine, but there is so much more. We cannot forget it was almost "modern times" when the barber surgeons were a guild—bound together by traditional practice and on the same social level as carpenters, goldsmiths, and shipwrights.

But back to the Chianciano Thermae area, almost certainly the site of <u>fontes clusini</u> (springs of Chuisi), made famous by the Emperor Augustus in the waning years of the first century B.C. Augustus was diagnosed with a liver abscess by his personal physician, Antonius Musa. The usual therapeutic interventions failed, so Dr. Musa advised partial submersion in the icy waters of the <u>fontes clusini</u>. We know this from the works of the Roman writer Horace, who believed in cold water treatments. (He used them to treat his chronic eye problems.)

Professor Soren's excavations in the cold water spring on the edge of Mezzomiglio are ongoing. During my most recent trip to Tuscany, I was able to wander around the excavated site, but several areas were covered with tarps and partially back-filled. I arrived too late in August—the archaeologists had finished their season two days before, according to the locals.

C. Le Thermae Montecatini

Montecatini is all about relaxation. Getting there is easy; it is just an hour and a half drive from Florence on the Florence-to-Mara superhighway. The town of Montecatini has about 20,000 inhabitants devoted to the spas. Strolling the streets around the central thermae, you find yourself in a typical Tuscan hill town, with small shops with wine, clothing, art, and trinkets for everyone's purse. If money is no object, there are Gucci and Cartier for shopping, and the Hotel La Pace for sleeping.

There are an estimated fifteen thousand hotel rooms and hundreds of small hotels from which to choose, and restaurants galore in every price range. If you must have your *Herald Tribune*, you will find it in a kiosk with all major European dailies. Clients are there to relax, and visitors like me are impressed with the quiet. No loud voices or boisterous tours or bambini are tolerated.

We entered the Thermae Tuccio, historically the most fashionable, where coat and tie for men and designer dresses for the women are de rigueur. You enter the tree-lined, shade-covered courtyard with manicured flower beds, and wafting in the air you hear a subdued string orchestra playing classical music of the seventeenth and eighteenth centuries. At a long marble table, brass spouts are labeled with the spring from whence each rises from the bowels of the earth. Rigina, Torretta, and Tettuccio are the Big Three. Each spout is labeled with therapeutic potential. Bowels, heart, kidneys, and central nervous system are the four major organ systems for which most visitors orally take the waters. There are specific waters for diuresis, constipation, arthritis, muscle weakness, and nervous disorders.

The atmosphere is conducive to total relaxation. If it were not for the soft classical music, the scene reminds me of the great musical *My Fair Lady*. A scene at the Ascot race course is performed in absolute silence, and those watching the race are shown in silhouette and slow motion as the horses go around the oval.

The spa offers mud baths, massage, immersion with and without exercise and colonics, just to mention a few. The seven major thermae in this area are Excelsior, Tetuccio, Leopoldine, Tamerici, Torretta, Redi, and La Salute. Woven into all this area are pharmacies for prescription and nonprescription medicine, and medical clinics for complete examinations and diagnostic laboratory workups. Even if you just stop for a brief visit, as we did, the diversion is worthwhile to enjoy the architecture. A few buildings dating to the Renaissance survived and many twentieth century art nouveau structures abound. Montecatini is recommended as a change of pace and respite from the hectic museum-ing of Florence and Pisa.

D. Casciano Thermae (Thermae di Casciano)

Casciano Thermae is a thoroughly modern facility without the Old World ambiance of Montecatini. However, it also is very accessible and lies south of the Arno River—northwest of Siena. If you are coming up A1 (Autostrada del Sole) in central Tuscany, go east on A11, and then pick up A12 south along the coast to the Casello di Lovorno turnoff, and soon Casciano appears.

The Thermae has modern bathing and exercise facilities in a Tuscan town environment. The thermae environs abound in hotels, rooming houses, and restaurants. We toured the facility and did not stay for any treatments, but were impressed with the cleanliness and organized efficiency. Again, there is a complete menu of spa interventions, including baths of different minerals, massage, pulmonary therapy for chronic lung disease, colonics and douches, kinetic muscle treatments, acupuncture, diuretic therapy, complete medical exams, pedicures, and manicures.

I was fascinated with their catalogs of creams and lotions. These include creams for treatment of wrinkles and prevention of wrinkles; post-bathing and detergent creams; astringent creams for use during the day, and separate concoctions for night use. For clients suffering from acne, hirsutism, solar sensitivity, and eczema, there are other combinations of ingredients. All in all, it is seemingly a well-run facility.

E. San Casciano dei Bagini

Our Tuscan summer home was near Certona. Just south of Monte Certona (Certona Mountain), in a wooden hill country dotted with vineyards, is San Casciano dei Bagini, a small spa town that we visited. There are no Etruscan attributes that I know of, but the Romans used it and I am certain the Etruscans did before them. Known today for helping with rheumatism, the hot spring provides private and group bathing, and mud baths and hotel rooms in a delightful rustic setting, overlooking rolling hills and vineyards—again, clean and inviting for use for a few hours to a week or more.

F. Chianciano Thermae

We will end this thermae section with a discussion of this historic site. This a large area with hundreds of hotels and rooming houses, and was probably very busy at least three millennia ago. If you enter the town, stay on the Viale della Libertá. If you are coming from the south, the resort and water facilities are to your right—east. Viale della Libertá runs along the ridge of the valley. To your left (west), up the hills, are all the hotels and rooming houses. To your right, as you look down into the valley, are the bathing facilities. The usual activities found in all complete Italian spas (as we have discussed before) are there, but here for the first time, as we discussed a few moments ago, Professor Soren of the University of Arizona has uncovered Etruscan baths.

The entire region is dotted with Etruscan sites. Almost anywhere you look, there is evidence of Etruscan culture. Tombs abound and archaeologists and antiquarians continue to find caches of ceramics, domestic, farming, and military artifacts. The commercial value of Chianciano Thermae today is huge, and surely provided business opportunities to the Etruscan and Roman entrepreneurs, who took care of the endless parade of the sick and injured, and who trooped to Chianciano (Fontes Clusini) in hope of relief from their bodily afflictions in this unforgiving world.

Finally, a recommendation to any traveler in this area: stop at the Etruscan Museum at the north end of town. This gem of a facility is located in an old granary, the basement of which is dug out of the tufa. The curator has very cleverly arranged reassembled tombs in the niches of the lower area, as they were found by the archaeologists. These three-dimensional displays are the best I have ever seen; they give the viewer a feel of what the discoverer of the tomb saw when he came upon the final resting place of the occupant, along with the possessions he took with him into the afterlife.

The small gift shop is excellent, with charges less than in Rome and Florence for similar items.

3

The North

A. Florence and Environs (Fiesole)

Florence—what more can a person possibly pen? When you visit this small metropolis as a tourist, Renaissance Florence is the center of gravity and, for most, the end-all.

From the late Middle Ages through at least the early Renaissance, Florence was the intellectual capital of the Italian peninsula. Truly, the Florence that radiates from the Ponte Vecchio—that grande dame straddling the Arno with her lifted skirts—is nothing more than an enormous indoor-outdoor museum. Every stone and arch has a story of love, murder, intrigue, creative genius, glory, and dashed hopes—mostly created during the fourteenth to sixteenth centuries A.D.

Lurking just below the paved surfaces can be found Etruscan and Roman Florence. Excavating is limited to small areas exposed at the time of modern water, sewer, and other utility projects, or when it is possible to look beneath the foundations of buildings under renovation. Recently, archaeology excavations in the Piazza della Signoria have identified pottery dating to the early Etruscan period of the eighth century B.C.

Beneath the Piazza della Signoria, at the tall, rectangular church of Orsanmichele, have been found votives—dedicated offerings to probably an unknown religious or cult center dating to the second century B.C.

The Mystery of the Tuscan Hills

The site is on Via di Cimatori, two blocks north of the Piazza della Signoria, parallel to the Piazza's northern edge that crosses Via del Calzoioli, the thoroughfare between Piazza della Signoria and Piazza Duomo, the site of the great cathedral (Duomo) and its bell tower (campanile) and the Baptistry of San Giovanni.

In the Piazza della Signoria, travelers' senses are overwhelmed with the art and architecture. The huge Loggia della Signori is my favorite sculpture space; it contains the bronze Perseus by Cellini as well as the Rape of the Sabine by Giambologna, and other equally priceless pieces.

The Palazzo Vecchio, the Florentine town hall, was the original site of Michelangelo's *David*, arguably the most recognized sculpture in the Western World. The *David* was commissioned by the City of Florence as a political symbol—representing the triumph of Republicanism over tyranny. Now, the original *David* resides in the Galleria dell' Academia, and in the summer of 2004 was restored to its original texture and color, and reopened to the public.

Close at hand are the Uffizi Gallery and the Pitti Palace—filled with so many treasures that a lifetime of study is needed to appreciate even a small portion of the art objects.

The point of this brief diversion is that when you walk in these spaces, your gaze is always uplifted, trying to take in almost more than your senses can absorb, surrounded as you are by the magnitude of the genius that blossomed in the fifteenth and sixteenth centuries.

But do not neglect the surface you are walking on, because just below the pavement stones, jumbled beneath new and ancient sewers and utility lines, are Etruscan and Roman remains—here, in the epicenter of the Renaissance, right in the navel of Florence. Clearly, the ancients recognized a good location (all real estate is location, location, location), near the Arno River and nestled in the bottom of a bowl formed by the surrounding hills.

There was a ford across the Arno near this site. The river at times is a quiet, meandering stream, but can become a mountain torrent following heavy rains in headwaters—witness the Great Flood of 1966 that washed over much of the ancient part of the city.

While in the area of the Piazza della Signoria, cross the Ponte Vecchio and walk to the east along the Lungarno Serristori. Then look to your right—that is, to the south—and a hill will appear called San Miniato al Monte. Here can be found several famous churches, but more importantly, near the summit is the Piazzale Michelangelo—a relatively quiet space with a spectacular view of the city and the orange ceramic roofs of countless structures, but dominated by the Duomo in all her splendor.

Only from this vantage point can you realize the immensity of this building dedicated to God. A panoramic view of the city from Fiesole, a town we will discuss shortly, is further away, and the city appears to be in miniature. But from the Piazzale Michelangelo, proportions seem more real. The walk to the top will take about an hour from the Piazza della Signoria, but is worth the effort—especially late in the afternoon with the western sun on the rooftops. If you are too tired, take a bus back (bus 13, I believe), and then you can enjoy a full dinner with pasta (try Ottarino on Via Della Oche, just one street south of the Duomo off the Via del Calzaiuole) and not feel guilty.

A "must" stop to view Etruscan art is the Museo Archeologico Number 38 on Via della Colonna. This nondescript building is on a rather rundown, grimy, narrow street with fast-moving traffic and narrow sidewalks. The street is like a canyon; the buildings all are three and four stories high, and mainly connected to each other. So when the motorcycles plummet down the street, the noise is deafening and multiplied in the canyon. But the walk is well worth the effort, since inside are three floors of Egyptian, Greek, Roman, and, of course, Etruscan antiquities.

The famous bronze Chimera from Arezzo (see Arezzo discussion in Part VI) is here, along with rooms of Greek vases of all styles and periods that were found in Etruscan tombs. The Etruscan collection has recently been refurbished. The 1966 flood made Via del Colonna a river, and the Etruscan collection that had been on the first floor at that time had to be restored and relocated in the museum. On display are the finest Etruscan jewelry and other arts—a must for anyone interested in the Classics, since the Greco-Roman-Egyptian collections are large and a postgraduate education in themselves.

If you make your way back to the Ponte Vecchio, the north end of the bridge is the Via Por Sante Maria. Follow this street north for one long block and you find yourself at Via Porta Rossa and the sixteenth century loggia of the Mercato Nuovo ("new market"). The open-air market is filled with low-price merchandise, peddled in the whole by gypsies.

In a "buyer beware" atmosphere, the Florentine Straw Market is formed by small stalls filled with leather goods, lace, and various trinkets. In the southeast corner of the market is a life-sized bronze boar (Il Porcellino) that supposedly will bring good luck by rubbing his nose, and is shiny from countless hands hoping for a bright future.

The Mercato Nuovo has a hidden story that has intrigued me for years. In fact, I spent almost five years researching a fascinating character (Charles Godfrey Leland), who lived in the shadow of the market and persuaded a gypsy sorceress, Maddelena, to help explain a little known aspect of Etruscan society—namely Etruscan medicine. I believe that you will enjoy the story of Charles Godfrey Leland, nicknamed "The Forgotten American." I will be as brief as possible during this diversion, but this was a true American genius, whose life and research findings were so important in understanding the early Etruscan culture. I promise it will not bore you.

Charles Godfrey Leland lived in the city of Philadelphia in the shadow of The Pennsylvania Hospital at the corner of Eighth and Spruce streets, where I had the good fortune to do my internship. Leland was born August 15, 1824, in Philadelphia, the son of a prominent Revolutionary family on both his mother's and father's sides, and died in Florence on March 20, 1903. Leland grew up at Third and Chestnut Streets, now Constitution Square, just a few blocks from The Pennsylvania Hospital. At age 20 months, Charles had a serious "meningitis-like" illness. Later in life, he credited the brain damage from that illness as being a significant factor in his nervousness, idealism, romanticism, poetic ability, and attraction to the occult and mysticism. Other significant influences included his sorceress Dutch nurse, who "cast several spells on him" when he was young.

Throughout his boyhood and developing years, Charles's interest in the occult increased. Later in life, he worked with gypsies in England and Southeastern Europe. At age six, he memorized

Prospero's speeches from Shakespeare's *The Tempest,* and he became a voracious reader at the Philadelphia Library, a private institution with 60,000 volumes in the 1830s. This membership was a gift from his father, who clearly recognized his son's hidden talents.

Charles Godfrey Leland's youth was almost idyllic. He went to a series of private schools in Philadelphia, and during the summer lived with his cousins in New England. Although he tended to be nervous and had a number of illnesses, he grew to be a six-foot-tall adult, who was vigorous except for occasional episodes of depression.

After three years at Princeton, where he was a maverick student, he was sent by his father to Heidelberg, Munich, and Paris for postgraduate studies. Here he developed the prototypical "student prince" life, as portrayed in Sigmund Romberg's famous opera of the same name. He returned to America in 1848 and stayed until 1862. During these years, he wrote hundreds of essays, reviews, and articles for the major periodicals of the time, including *Vanity Fair, Graham's Magazine* and the *Knickerbocker Magazine.* In the 1850s and during the Civil War, he had strong pro-union sentiments.

During an explosion of creativity, he produced a series of humorous and satirical German-English dialect poems, modeled after the German-English immigrants living in Philadelphia. His ear for words and sounds was as fine-tuned as any opera singer, and the series soon made Leland a wealthy man, with his fictional character "Hans Breitman." He was ostracized by the academic community, as he had been ostracized at Princeton, for not being scientific enough or sufficiently scholarly. He also was regarded as being too far ahead of their mechanistic world. Nevertheless, he continued to delve into the occult. The income from the Hans Breitman sales, and an inheritance from his father, enabled him to pursue his studies independently.

He studied Algonquin Indian legends and myths, became a great folklorist and a social anthropologist seventy-five years before Margaret Mead did her great work. Leland did an impressive amount of field work. He lived with Indian groups for months at a time and recorded their stories, cross-checking with various sources. He also studies the myths of the Eskimos, a number of Finnish and Laplander groups, and various Mongoloid peoples. He found parallels between the themes in various Norse Eddas and North American Indian myths, and saw that many of the Algonquin stories could be related to the Norse legends. He postulated certain themes diffused from Greenland down to Canada and into Northeast America.

Leland's studies included postgraduate work in Germany, which led him to the conviction that the United States did not have a legitimate folk ethos. He maintained that American Indians understood nature and spirituality even better than Emerson or Whitman.

His works preceded Joseph Campbell's famous mythological writing of the mid-twentieth century by about a hundred years.

Leland's writings covered other diverse topics. His book on willpower explained how he had been able to strengthen his mind and memory through self-hypnosis. While in Philadelphia, he developed a manual art system of instruction in the Philadelphia school system that remained in place for about one hundred years. During an extended stay in the American West, he lived with the Crow Indians and also reviewed the flourishing world of pulp literature about the Far West that had flowed into the Northeast.

In 1856, at age 32, Leland published *The Poetry and Mystery of Dreams* that predated Sigmund Freud's work by about fifty years. He admired poets for their understanding of the imagery of dreams, and for their imaginations, most of which they were able to correlate with the drama of real life. In addition, he discussed ancient Greek and Arab writers' work on dreams.

Charles Godfrey Leland then traveled with the gypsies in England and published the definitive dictionary of the gypsy language. He looked at the gypsies' origin from India and identified their language (Shelta) in England as a tongue used by itinerant tinkers as an ancient Celtic language. He also wrote the definitive dictionary of the Celtic dialect. Leland traveled throughout Eastern Europe with various gypsy groups and finally settled in Florence, where he stayed for a number of years to study the witches (stregas) of northern Italy. During the next twenty busy years, Leland translated twenty volumes of the German poet Heinrich Heine and wrote a total of fifty volumes of the Hans Breitman series.

It was fun for me to follow the narrow streets and alleys in Florence where Leland walked and talked and listened. He talked to the gypsies in the Mercato for years, especially to the witch,

Maddelena, who confided in Leland the secrets of the medical treatments performed by the witches in the countryside.

In 1849, the Brothers Grimm founded in an obscure archive in Germany a book of 100 Magical Cures, current in the rural classes of Tuscany in the fourth and fifth centuries A.D. This was compiled by Marcellus Burdigalensis, a court physician to the late Roman emperor Flavius Honorius (384 to 423 A.D.). Honorius was the son of Theodosius I. He was young and feeble when made emperor, and was constantly looking for medical help. He commissioned his court physician to find from the stregas, or witches, in northern Italy, possible cures for his illnesses.

These charms, recorded by Burdigalensis, were ancient at this time and were felt to be Etruscan or earlier in origin. Leland found that even at the end of the nineteenth and the beginning of the twentieth century, many of these age-old treatments were still in use by the witches. They included phantasmagorical treatments for dreams, toothaches, various eye problems, all types of bodily pains, bladder stones, and colic. The pharmacology involved an enormous number of herbs, various animal parts, charms, incantations, and mumbo-jumbo phrases.

After years of talking with Maddelena, Leland pieced together the original "Etruscan remedies," used as far back as the seventh century B.C. It is unfortunate that Leland has been forgotten in the academic centers in America. He was truly a multifaceted and brilliant thinker, but in his own time, thought "not to be scientific enough" and soon forgotten. He made original contributions in anthropology, psychology, ethnology, and to the history of medicine and literature.

Some day, hopefully he will take his rightful place in American letters.

So, even a small, seemingly insignificant gypsy straw market can have a great story!

A brief excursion to the environs of Florence is in order; in fact, it is a must. The hilltop town of Fiesole is our destination—about eight kilometers northeast from the heart of Florence. Fiesole, now a town of about fourteen thousand, is easily accessed by bus or car, and has a panoramic view of Florentine rooftops and, of course, the Duomo.

I commented on the immensity of this structure before, but when you see it from Fiesole, the true perspective is apparent. I have climbed to the top of the Duomo's dome, designed by Filippo Brunelleschi. The dome is a double shell, and the climber ascends between the shells through an elaborate series of narrow stairs. You pop out at the apex onto a narrow ledge with a protective rail that does a 360 degree giro, and spread out before you is Florence. I have climbed the Duomo in Milan, St. Mark's in Venice, St. Peter's in Rome, Montheale in Palermo, just to name a few. As you stand on the skin of these structures, they never seem as large as when you see them from afar and above; this also is the case with the Duomo of Florence when seen from Fiesole.

Fiesole to me is a grove—albeit a giant grove, since the hill is heavily wooded and has attracted families and clans since before the Bronze Age (second and third millennia B.C.), and in the Iron Age (1000 B.C.), was a Villanovan settlement before it became an Etruscan city. Fiesole (Latin: Faesulae; Etruscan: Vipsul) was one of the chief cities of the Etruscan confederacy and dates, most believe, to the fifth or sixth century B.C. The climate in Fiesole is more temperate than in Florence in the summer months, so wealthy Florentines have always lived there.

The Romans defeated the Etruscans and made Fiesole an important city for centuries, and actually dominated Florence until a battle in 1125 A.D., when Fiesole slowly sank into obscurity politically. But to this day, it remains a delightful place to live. The hilltop position made it an important defensive military site, since the citizens could easily control the Arno River traffic, and there is, as well, a major ford. The city has many villas and hidden gardens that are difficult for the visitor to explore, since many of them have been occupied for the past 150 years by expatriate Britishers with Victorian trust funds, and wealthy American savants and pseudo-intellectuals with Gilded Age parents and grandparents who accumulated large fortunes that lasted through their non-working descendants' lives.

The Roman theatre and accompanying baths, built into the side of the hill and nearby Etruscan museum, afford the tourist devoted to the classics an interesting day. The theatre held three thousand spectators. A terrace above the excavation gives the viewer a brief but understanding view of the architectural layout of this Roman civic and entertainment center. There are remnants of an Etruscan city wall of substantial length with a ruined gate. The Museo Bandini, just to the right of the entrance of the Roman theatre, has Etruscan vases and other modest works of art found in the vicinity.

The museum has a collection of artifacts from all the peoples that occupied Fiesole, to enjoy in a quiet and unhurried way. The main Etruscan cult site was on the north slope, where bronze votive figurines were found. Beneath the Roman temple was found traces of an Etruscan temple—perhaps dedicated to the goddess Minerva.

4

The Northwest

A. San Gimignano

San Gimignano is my least favorite Tuscan hilltop town; in fact, I can almost say I abhor this tourist trap, crowded with unruly crowds in the summer months. This reasonably preserved medieval town attracts, on any given summer weekend, many more thousands than the 7,000 permanent residents. They come to gawk at the thirteen remaining phallic towers (originally 76) built by wealthy families in the medieval centuries—presumably to hide the family jewels and virgin daughters. This hilltop was, of course, an Etruscan settlement, but it is hopelessly covered with Roman and extant medieval buildings.

The museums are filled with Middle Ages and Renaissance art, and nary a major Etruscan artifact. Enough of San Gimignano—not a worthwhile stop for those looking for the Etruscans.

B. Pisa

Pisa is almost impossible to enjoy. The town lies in a strategic site near the mouth of the Arno River, and was a great trading center in Etruscan and Roman times. It probably was used by Iron Age folk as distant as 1000 B.C. Again, Pisa simply is difficult to enjoy because of the thousands of tourists who flock to the Piazza del Duomo on a greensward, containing the cathedral, Leaning Tower, and Baptistry.

I have an image of a fish trap in a river with a large opening that slowly narrows as the fish swims forward. Finally the net becomes too narrow for the fish to turn around.

This is Pisa, with a host of roads leading into the city and the tourist-fish rushing to the narrow Piazza del Duomo, where, at noon on a July or August day, it is difficult to turn around. However, all must attend this small space—so important in western art and civilization. Like a baited fish trap, along one side of the Piazza are several hundred kiosks, hawking every known religious and secular artifact ever produced in Italy.

But what of the Etruscans? In the Archaic (sixth to fifth centuries B.C.), Pisa was one of the principal Etruscan cities. Geography, plus local mines, quarries, and forests, made Pisan families wealthy. The cemeteries have been studied and Pisa's trading connections to the north verified. My recommendation: make your mandatory pilgrimage to see the Leaning Tower, but do not waste time on Etruscan remnants.

C. Volterra (Etruscan: Velathri; Latin: Volaterrae)

Volterra is a must-visit if one is to understand Etruscan city life, and an opportunity to visit a first-rate regional museum whose rooms are filled with the personal collections of eighteenth century antiquarians that form the nucleus of this collection.

Perfectly situated on a hill, dominating the Cecina and Era River valleys (a prime piece of real estate since Villanovan days in the tenth century B.C.), this was the northern-most part of the Etruscan confederation of city-states.

Volterra offers much to enjoy, and I find it difficult to know where to begin. Several streets lead to the top of the hill—crowned with the Duomo as her tiara. Mixed in with a myriad of churches are extensive Etruscan and Roman venues. On the south side, near the convenient underground parking garage, is the Archaeology Park (Parco Archeologio) and the famous Arco Etrusco (Etruscan Arch). On the north side is found the magnificent Roman theater and baths, rarely overcrowded, with a chance to view from above. Descending to the stage allows the full impact of a Roman theater. In the very

The Mystery of the Tuscan Hills

northeast corner of the city are the Etruscan walls—outside of the medieval walls. Nestled inside the medieval walls in the northeast area is the Museo Etrusco Guarnicci. The city is blessed with several other fine museums, but we will limit our comments to the Etruscan museum.

The archaelogy park is a public garden on the Etruscan and subsequent Roman acropolis. The very important and beautiful Etruscan gateway (Arco Etrusco/Porta all' Arco) was erected in the fourth to third century B.C. The three monumental heads—presumably Etruscan deities, but never firmly established—still stare down on the visitor and welcome him to the city. Enter the gate and gradually walk up the steep street, trying to take in all the history that has preceded your visit, and you will soon find yourself in a maze of streets leading to the center of town.

The Guarnicci Museum houses one of the best collections in all of Etruria. The eighteenth century private collection of Frances Chini in the Guarnicci forms much of the nucleus of the museum, but much material has been added over the past three hundred years. The museum has a full complement of cinerary urns, jewelry, bronze figurines, and lamps. This is a must stop.

Volterra's funerary art gives even the casual observer a picture of life of the aristocracy. In large, complex tombs, and multiple rooms inside chambers, has been found evidence of the role of the paternal oligarch: as businessman, priest, and lawyer. Arguably the most important of the Volterran tombs are the elaborate cinerary arms of the Inghirami family, in the Ultemeto Necropolis.

Many of the tombs in and about Volterra are accessible without a guide, but finding a local will help immensely in sorting out the important areas of the cemeteries. Take a flashlight, since the tombs are not lit, as those in Tarquinia are.

Take time along the way to absorb all the visions flooding your senses every second of the day. In July and August, the sky is usually cloudless and the sun is bright—giving these small hill towns and villages different earth tones every hour of the day.

I am most attracted to the end of the day, as the sun slowly settles in the west. Then the sienna roof tiles darken and the shadows on the hills lengthen, making lone trees, ruined castles, and monasteries seem etched by a fine master engraver.

During the height of the day, take special care to enjoy the panorama of wildflowers in the July and August months. The poppies—best in June—are fading, but the yellowbroom, found in huge patches or as an isolated plant protruding from behind a rock, is in full bloom. My favorite is the reddish-purple vetch, also in full array. The grapevines are filling out as they climb the hillsides and cap the apex of their domain; even with the noon-time sun, they appear hazy in the distance.

5

North Central

A. Siena

Siena is my favorite city in all of Italy—end of discussion! Everyone who travels to Italy has his or her favorite town. Some will argue for Rome, Florence, or Venice, but this is like a discussion of whether you are a New York Yankee, Boston Red Sox, or San Francisco Giant fan. Your loyalty and attraction have nothing to do with facts and logic; they are purely emotional and subjective.

Siena is like a stately Victorian dowager trying to live in the twentieth century. Nothing can change her mind about dress, or her attitude toward a rapidly altering world. You enter Siena and immediately step back into the fifteenth or sixteenth century. Sixteenth century Sienese citizens would have no trouble adjusting to Siena in 2004 and, in fact, would immediately pick up where they left off three or four hundred years ago.

The same food and many of the major buildings exist inside the city walls, including the Duomo and Il Campo (the Great Public Space), where the famous Il Palio horse race is held in July and August. I know Siena so well that I probably could fill fifty pages, but we need to stick to our Etruscan task at hand.

In Siena, you will see Rome's symbol of the she-wolf, suckling the twins Romulus and Remus.

Legend has it that the sons of Remus—Senius and Ascius—founded Siena. Siena's flag is one half white and one half black; Senius rode a black steed and Ascius a white horse.

Siena sits on a Y-shaped ridge and spreads out onto the sides of the ridges into the shallow valley. In Siena, the streets and alleys are constantly going either up or down or around the central piazza (Il Campo). Before Senius and Ascius, the Etruscans lived on this ridge top. Excavations over the past hundred years have found traces of Etruscan habitation—surely more is hidden beneath Roman Siena (Saena Iulia), and the nine hundred years of Medieval Renaissance and contemporary Siena.

During the Renaissance period, Etruscan tombs and inscriptions were found, and studied with little scholarship by the humanists who described them. In the eighteenth century, excavations by antiquarians of several classic Etruscan sites stimulated an early interest in the Etruscans. In the mid-nineteenth century, after the united Italian state was formed, Etruscan studies rapidly expanded and museums were opened throughout the country, including a modest collection in Siena with artifacts from the nearby tombs—none of them to my knowledge scientifically excavated.

In the Siena region, scattered villages surrounded the hilltop area. If there was a significant Etruscan town, no record comes down to us. The first urban settlement was during Roman times, during Augustus's reign, at the end of the Etruscan civilization.

I end my brief visit to Siena with a few more thoughts. The best way to tackle Siena is to head directly to the Il Campo (in my mind, the best public space ever devised by city architects). The piazza is slightly sloped and is in the form of a fan, or scallop shell, and was once the Roman Forum, it is said. But the slope reminds me more of a Roman amphitheater.

Everything worth seeing radiates off the Il Campo. At the base of the piazza, where it is flat, resides the Palazzo Publico, filled with rooms of Sienese art. If you don't mind heights, climb the adjacent campanile (bell tower). The Duomo museum in the Palazzo Bon Signori is the most important gallery for study of Sienese masters. This area is reached by leaving the southwest corner of Il Campo. I also recommend trying the northwest corner, toward the large Gothic church San Francesco. Look for Via della Sapienza and the entrance to the Biblioteca Comunale.

In this rather auspicious building is a library with more than one hundred thousand volumes, and laced with rare illuminated missals, breviaries, and Books of Hours. My adrenaline gets flowing when I see the rare book bindings. Every year for several centuries, one artist was given the commission by the city fathers to design a book cover for the minutes of all civic deliberations of the previous year. Many of these are on permanent display, and each a work of art. For a book lover like myself, this is heaven on earth.

Adjoining the library are eleven rooms of the Museo Archaeologico Etrusco (Etruscan Archaeology Museum), with Etruscan and Roman finds from the tombs surrounding the area. Included is the Bargagli family collection from Sarteano—the town nearest to our summer farmhouse retreat of 2002, and just a few miles from Siena. Remember, even in July and August, when Rome, Pisa, Florence, and Venice are packed with sweaty tourists shoulder to shoulder—and elbowing each other to get a better view of a painting in the Pitti Palace or bribing the maitre d' to get a table in a decent restaurant—Siena is there for the taking. Housing and food are never a problem.

Spend the late afternoon and early evening strolling the streets above the Il Campo, window shopping, and stopping for a gelato or espresso—and then finding a table at one of the many open-air cafes at the top of Il Campo for a glass of vino or campari and soda.

If you are there in July or August, and it is the week before the Il Palio (the wildest and craziest horse race in the world), the contrata, or neighborhood, flag teams will be parading around the Il Campo, waving huge flags on long staffs and drumming up support for their horse and jockey. The Il Palio is different than horse racing in America. Each contrata, or neighborhood, has its own church and club that dates back several hundred years. Inside the building are the jockey's silks worn when the horse of that contrata won the race. What is different than in America is that the city of Siena controls the horses, and the jockeys belong to each contrata. There is an enormous amount of betting, and fierce, emotional competition between the contratas. Regardless of where you live at this time, if you were born in a certain contrata, that is yours for the rest of your life.

For one day in July and one day in August, Il Campo is filled with dirt and sand to create a racetrack. The horses circumvent the course twice, and with no holds barred. The center of Il Campo is filled with spectators and all the buildings that surround the piazza are filled with dignitaries hanging from the balconies and windows.

Remember, Siena is always manageable, courteous, and—importantly—fairly priced. Only on Il Palio days does the tourist run the risk of being trampled emotionally and physically.

B. Tenuta (Farm Estate) di Spannocchia and La Piana

The mist slowly dissipates in the valley below an hour or so after sunrise. Brown patches blend in with the green of low foliage. The brown is harvested grains or mown grasses adjacent to green areas yet to be invaded by farm machinery. In the morning, there is not much animal life to view. The deer have retreated to their glade. Birds swoop after invisible creatures in the air, and raptors soar on warm drafts, seeking a wounded rabbit or unsuspecting rodent. But return an hour or so before sunset, when the shadows begin to drape over the edges of the valley like a cotton scarf on the sagging shoulders of an ancient, gnarled, kyphotic peasant nonna.

Be patient, because with a bit of good fortune, the wild pigs will come out of the shelter of an oak copse and begin to forage for the evening meal. The sow comes first, followed in single file by five to eight piglets. The boar often is seen protecting their flank. At a distance of one-fourth to one-half mile, they are oblivious to you, and with a glass of wine and a piece of cheese, you can enter into their world of dining. This scene can be repeated at any hilltop villa; it was first witnessed by me at the Tenuta di Spannocchia in 1982 and later described in the beginning of this piece at our 2003 farmhouse villa at Abbazia di Speneto.

The Tenuta di Spannocchia is a very special place and institution. Spannocchia is owned by a successful Italian-American businessman and his family. I do not know the property's exact date of construction, but it was founded by one of the original banking families in Siena. The bell in the bell tower was cast in 1492—the year Columbus sailed for America. Spannocchia is now a non-profit institution devoted to the study of Italian culture, with its primary emphasis on the Etruscans. The Etruscan Foundation coordinates and administers programs at Spannocchia. Activities over the years on this estate of several thousand acres, in addition to the very important Etruscan excavation at La Piana, include the study of an ancient nunnery and a castle from the Middle Ages, in addition to numerous conferences in art history and the classics.

Several buildings of note can be found on the estate. The restored farm houses built in the sixteenth and seventeenth centuries are examples of Tuscan rural architecture. They are basic brick in structure, with a large kitchen and a huge fireplace. The castle is named Castel che deo Sol Sa ("The Castle Only God Knows"), whose foundation dates to the tenth century. Apparently, it was built by a Scottish knight who fought with Charlemagne. When I last saw the structure, it was in a state of disrepair but there were plans to preserve it and keep the stonework from further erosion.

On the property is the Ponte della Pia, a Roman bridge of beautiful proportions. It leads to the top of a hill, where the St. Lucia Nunnery sits. The story of the bridge is one of two important Sienese families in the thirteenth century. A marriage ensued and the wife cheated on her husband. He found out and sent her to a tower on the coast for life. There she died. Her name was Pia and she crossed this bridge while spending the night in the nunnery on the way to the tower.

One ascends what is probably the remnants of the Roman Road to the nunnery of St. Lucia. There is found a ruined Romanesque church and the convent. The latter structure is said to have had its sculpture removed and sold to the Berlin Museum. This is also a Roman site, proven by an earlier dig.

The Etruscan Foundation[1] is dedicated to "the conservation, documentation, preservation, and restoration of the natural and cultural heritage of Tuscany and ancient land of the Etruscans." Activities now include study of the ecosystem with organic farming practices, study of regional architecture, and all cultural and material Etruscan history. The Etruscan Foundation advisory board publishes

---

1. The Etruscan Foundation's web site is office@etruscanfoundation.org. Its field headquarters site is field@etruscanfoundation.org.

Etruscan Studies, the only journal in English totally devoted to Etruscology.

The physical layout of Spannocchia is like the villa rustica, or Roman farm, of a wealthy, landed aristocratic family. Villa rusticas are found throughout the Roman Empire; they were a vital ingredient in holding together Rome's vast territories, both economically and politically. In general terms, they include the owner's personal home (villa) and adjacent farm buildings, workshops and peasant housing—in Roman times, primarily slaves and a scattering of freed men. Spannocchia has all these architectural elements; in the past it was probably an Etruscan farm and then a Roman villa rustica. When I was an excavator under the aegis of Professor Jane Whitehead, the diggers ("grunts") lived in a dormitory-like building, modified from former barns, stables, and workshops. In close proximity to the villa are the tenant farmhouses. The family members are cooks and servants to the big house, and also perform all the chores and duties of a working farm.

Spannocchia is just a few kilometers southwest of Siena, near the village of Rosia. You approach the villa from a rather shallow and narrow valley, between the verdant hills, with outcroppings of marble and tufa. The villa is beautifully sited on the hilltop, with a winding road that leisurely guides you from the valley floor to the main house. As the road must make several bends, the views of the villa vary as you approach, with the ubiquitous cypress trees as a greeting and standing guard along the road to the main house. The roadway widens into a courtyard and a modest architectural home greets you—along with a friendly dog or two.

Spannocchia is not an elaborate structure with formal gardens of any magnitude, as portrayed in the coffee-table books beckoning the reader to the villas of Tuscany, filled with baroque chapels, garden statuary, and faux Roman wall painting.

The main family house when I was there was simply decorated with sturdy, provincial furniture. The kitchen was a marvel of non-mechanical food production—no fancy ovens, dishwashers, refrigerators, or mixers—but the meals and bread for hungry archaeologists and classics students were marvelous.

I best remember the gigantic fireplace, with seats along the sides to keep warm in the dank spring and fall days, and cold winter evenings.

Even in the summer, the fire burned brightly when a cool breeze blew across the hilltop after the sun went down, and it was trying to rain or drizzle. The group would gather around the fireplace, exchanging ideas about the archaeology finds of that day and learning about each other.

If you keep your antennae turned on and focus, the sounds and activities of the tenant farmers—some of whom live in the cottage adjacent to the housing for the students—reveal another world, which I could only realize from the fringe. I used to sit on the low stone wall that separated our housing from the cottages and try to eavesdrop, including hearing every afternoon the strega "talking chicken" to her birds and scattering corn, which their bobbing heads greedily pecked off the cottage front yard.

A few kilometers from Spannocchia, and not on the farm property, lies a small Etruscan site: La Piana. Like most Etruscan settlements, a flat surface on top of a hill was chosen. It overlooks the Merse River flood plain, with soil to this day fertile enough to produce food for a large population. La Piana is an important dig, since there are precious few excavated provincial Etruscan sites. Murlo, discussed in the next section, is a provincial community, but its large workshop area produced high-quality goods and was much larger and more sophisticated than La Piana.

The point is, in past years, almost all Etruscan archaeology has been the exposure and study of tombs and large urban sites. La Piana is tiny, but Professor Jane Whitehead, expertly and laboriously over a decade, deciphered this small community and early on provided one of the few windows into rural Etruscan life. Currently, there is more interest in this area, and over the next twenty or thirty years, the daily life of the Etruscan will be peeled off, layer by layer, from the soil of these small habitations. La Piana's families lived in a self-contained environment, with evidence of such domestic activity as weaving.

The farmland at the base of the hill provided an abundance of food. Professor Whitehead has shown that La Piana met its end in the third century B.C. The community was burned to the ground after an assault, using small ballistic missiles, and was never rebuilt or re-inhabited. In some recent articles discussing Etruscan farming communities, La Piana has been neglected. This oversight needs correcting, because the skill and accuracy of this excavation exceeds any thus far published, as far as I have been able to read.

C. Murlo

Murlo is included in this book because of the area's importance in Etruscan culture. This is a rural area and differs in several ways from the more urban Etruscan centers emphasized in guide books. A visit to the Murlo Museum is the main reason for visiting this site. The active archaeological zone is off-limits, but is a wonderful walk from the roadside if you are fortunate to find excavators at work. The drive to Murlo through the countryside is relaxing, with a slow climb to the top of this hill town.

When you arrive at the small museum, a treat is in store for you. The archaeological finds are displayed in a way the visitor can appreciate Etruscan artistic genius. A section of the roof covering an Etruscan building has been restored and is capped with the famous terra cotta (sixth century B.C.) acroterial bearded man with the Texas cowboy hat.

The Murlo site, like most Etruscan ruins, is a foundation with the roof tumbled down, since walls were of mud and plaster and the roof supported by wooden poles—long since turned to dust. At Murlo, fire destroyed several major buildings; this preserved, under the ashes in the dust and debris brought in by the wind and rain, enough information to reconstruct a vibrant, rural, aristocratic community with workshops. So even if the site were open to the public, no significant architectural features remain above ground.

Along the edge (revetment) of one of the major buildings was a terra cotta frieze. Fragments of the frieze have been found and pieced together like a giant jigsaw puzzle. Art historians have studied the reconstructed shards, and much has been written of their meaning. Questions, as always, remain, but what was very obvious was that women in this rural Etruscan setting had equal status with men.

Earlier, I discussed the modeled husband and wife, reclining in each other's arms on the lid of their sarcophagus. The Murlo frieze is not a death scene, but an actual banquet of an obviously wealthy and perhaps aristocratic family, with the women lying on dining couches, in equal status with the men.

Also shown is a couple in a horse-drawn carriage sitting side by side. In Rome at this time, the only women allowed in a carriage were the Vestal Virgins, and they, of course, did not ride beside a man. Also, Roman men dined alone. Greek society forbade women to participate in banquets with their spouses and other male family members. The female figures we see on Greek vases at special occasions are prostitutes.

A visit to Murlo is not too time consuming, and you might consider adding Murlo to a day excursion after a trip to the Abbazia di Monte Oliveto Maggiora—but only if your visit to the Abbazia is not too long. The Abbazia is 27 kilometers (17 miles) southeast of Siena. Instead of heading back to Siena, go west on the S2 Road (Via Cassia) to Vescovado. Then follow the signs (2 km–1 mi) to Murlo. The museum (Antiquariam Poggio Civitte) is in a lovely building that was once a bishop's palace.

If the roof tiles and terra cotta cowboys don't excite you like they do me, then the museum has beautifully displayed gold, bronze, silver, and ivory decorative pieces. Some of these small masterpieces are imported, and reveal extensive trade routes between Poggio Civitte and other regions of the Italian peninsula—and even other countries.

If you are really compulsive on the road to Murlo, look for Sovana—a small Etruscan site on the usual tufa plateau with extensive fourth through second century B.C. tufa rock-cut tombs.

D. Monte Oliveto Maggiora Monastery

While we are in the area of Murlo, a stop at, and a few comments about, the Monte Oliveto are in order. The most visited monastery in all of Italy, it is an oasis of olive and cypress trees, carefully groomed with walking pathways and areas in which to sit and contemplate the universe. The site was founded in 1313 by Giovanni Tolomei, a rich Sienese lawyer who began the Oliveto order, a branch of the Benedictines.

The monastery is in the La Crete region of Etruscan country, but as far as I know, no significant Etruscan finds have been unearthed on the monastery grounds. Please don't let this deter you if you are a lover of Renaissance architecture. The abbey church is only so-so in my eyes, but the graceful gate house is worth the visit. Take a deep breath and relax for an hour or so in the cypress woods, and then make your way to the La Torre Ristorante, situated on a beautiful patio near the gatehouse. A bottle of the local wine and a pasta entrée, I guarantee, will make your arrival at your hotel later than you anticipated.

Remember to ask if the book building is open. The Abbazia is dedicated to book restoration. If indeed I get recycled, I will ask for a position in the restoration department. The sixteenth century library has forty thousand volumes, and some day I hope to return and see the room which is situated inside the church compound, near the refractory. Remember to take time to walk through the pine and cypress pathways and stop in the grotto to pray and reorganize your thoughts—a good time to reprioritize your life.

E. Grosetto/Rusellae

Grosetto is a modest town of about seventy thousand inhabitants who live in the coastal plains south of Pisa and west and a bit north of Lake Bolsena. Grosetto lies in the Maremma—the area of Italy ravaged for centuries by malaria, especially during Roman times and the Middle Ages.

The Etruscans, the great engineers and public health advocates, undoubtedly drained the marshes and swamps into a shallow gulf. The Etruscan towns of Vetulonia and Rusellae were built upon the highest points of two islets. Over the centuries, the bay silted in. The original Etruscan towns were of the Etruscan confederation city states. Roman occupation was extensive, but in 935 A.D., the Saracen invaders destroyed the site, and it was never rebuilt because of malaria epidemics.

About eight kilometers northeast of Grosetto is the small spa of Roselle Thermae, still in use near a host of medieval ruins.

In Grosetto, inside the walled medieval city, is found the Duomo with a small museum (Museo Archaeologico a D'arte Della Maremma) with a smattering of Etruscan and Roman antiquities from the surrounding area. (The most famous piece is a black bowl with the twenty-two Etruscan alphabet letters scratched on the surface.) During the Archaic period of Etruscan history, about 575 to 480 B.C., Roselle (Latin) Rusellae and its adjacent islet city state Vetulonia (Etruscan: Vetlunia, Vathina) were at their height.

Richly-furnished sixth century B.C. tombs in Vetulonia are silent witness to her wealth and influence on the coast, but the lagoon silted in and she slowly slipped into oblivion. However, Roselle is worth pursuing because it is a pleasant site to leisurely walk about. A good guide is a necessity because of the jumble of stones, and it takes a local expert to identify the Roman and Etruscan structures—not always obvious to the unfamiliar eye. The guides know every stone, of which there are many.

The remains of a massive mud brick city wall and later stone walls will be your most impressive memory of the site, along with the view into the valley below that stretches out to the sea. This is real estate with a view—location, location, location! The remains include early Etruscan houses, including the most famous one, designed to collect its own water for bathing, cooking, and drinking. The entire complex is about 20 hectares (45 acres) and encircles an area greater than one-half mile. Only a small fraction of the site has been excavated in a scientific fashion, but those areas exposed reveal:

- An archaic Etruscan temple
- Etruscan and Hellenistic pottery kilns
- A huge Roman cistern
- An entry to the site on an old Roman road
- A Roman basilica
- A Roman forum
- A Roman villa with mosaic floors and drainage
- A complex site drainage system

Morris M. Weiss, M.D.

By the time you have trundled about Roselle, hopefully on a blue-sky, July Etruscan summer day, sit down and smell the fennel and other wildflowers, and watch the birds float on the warm air drafts. If the time is early to mid-afternoon, don't rush back to Grosetto to see the Duomo Museum if you missed it earlier—it will probably be closed anyway. Instead, follow the road down the hill and go for a swim on the beach. Then—with a piece of cheese, some hard bread, and a bottle of the local vino—watch the sun move to her bed in the west.

6

The Northeast

A. Arezzo (Latin: Arretium)

Arezzo is one of the principal autonomous Etruscan cities. This low hilltop town has recognizable archaeological evidence dating back to the Iron Age (Villanova period), from before 1000 B.C. Arezzo is five kilometers south of the eastern reaches of the Arno River. To the west, along the Arno, just before it empties into the Mediterranean, is Pisa, and in midcourse of this important water highway is Florence.

This geographic location has meant, since before written history, that Arezzo's site is strategically important. In 1869, near the gate (named for a local fountain—Fonte Venezia), were excavated 180 bronze figures and assorted terra cotta votive offerings to an unknown Etruscan deity. This was a healing center, since the ex-voto pieces were modelled in the shape of various body parts in need of healing (head, eyes, legs, among others). The Etruscan Arezzo, which thrived from the seventh to the fourth century B.C., was wealthy, with a metal industry, farming, and a red-glaze pottery (Arrentine ware) that was traded all over the then-known world.

According to Livy, during the Roman period in the third century B.C., the city submitted to Rome and, after a citizen revolt, Rome restored the aristocratic Clinii clan to power, presumably on the condition that it remain a loyal client of Rome. Roman Arezzo remained as wealthy and productive as the Etruscan city for centuries, into the Middle Ages.

The best way to approach Arezzo, a city that resembles any small town, is to find a parking space at the base of her hill. The area around Arezzo, when you first enter the city, is a rather colorless landscape of light industry and drab buildings. So park, and slowly ascend the first street of any width that you see. After a few minutes' walk, you will reach the top of the city that opens into a broad piazza—the unspoiled part of the city. Most tourists eventually find the Church of San Francesco and the Duomo (cathedral), which are worth a brief giro.

Arezzo is a walled, medieval city with remnants of Roman, even Etruscan, walls. The Roman amphitheater and modest archaeology museum are on the south side. Arguably the most important bronze Etruscan sculpture is the Chimera, an Etruscan casting of the fifth century B.C. This fantastical animal has the body of a lion, the head of a ram on its back, and a serpent's tail. It is found in room XIV in the Museo Archeologio (Museum of Archaeology) in Florence. Also from Arezzo, in the same room, is the bronze Minerva, a copy of a fifth century Greek work.

Arezzo is known for a wonderful antique fair that begins in the Grand Piazza at the top of the hill on the first Sunday of every month, but actually begins on Saturday, since a general market is held every Saturday. Slowly climb to the hilltop, absorbing the city as you go, to get the lay of the land and the arrangement of goods and merchants. When you reach the top, in the large open space, the major antique open-air bourses are found. From the pate of the hill, streets draping like cornrows descend the sides of the hill and flow to the shoulders of the city.

You'll find the goods of hundreds of merchants, selling everything from expensive antique furniture, fixtures, and paintings, to simple buttons and modern knockoffs, with a melange of T-shirts and pirated music kiosks. There is something for any purse and momentary whimsy.

We visited Arezzo on a Fair Day and, as we came back down the hill and reached our car, we found that the driver's side window had been smashed into thousands of tiny shards. Someone must have hit it with a crowbar or a medium-sized hammer. Glass was on the street and inside the car. As if by a miracle, around the corner of the building came two police officers—one male and one female—who were quite polite and, in their very flowery, Italian way, said they had never seen anything like this happen before in their city.

However, the male officer took his walkie-talkie off his belt and, within seconds, as though it had been waiting around the corner, this wonderful little white truck appeared. Two technicians jumped out, in red jumpsuits, opened the back of the truck and appeared with a vacuum cleaner that was attached to a motor inside the truck. Again within seconds, they had all the glass suctioned off the street and out of the car. Clearly, this was not a rare event in Arezzo. I made the mistake of leaving my international cell phone between the seats, near the gear shift, and clearly, the people who broke into the car had seen it. But that was just the beginning of our fun, since the car was, of course, rented, and we now needed a new car. We got into the car and followed the police to the local substation.

Then began such a wonderful comedy that I am sorry I did not have a video camera and tape recorder to reproduce it. In any case, the police needed our passports and said they would call the rental people, who had an office in Arezzo. But after many phone calls, they found out that the Arezzo office was closed and the car would have to be returned to the airport in Florence, where it was originally rented. There was a series of phone calls, discussions, and the filling out of multiple documents that had to be attested to by us, including such wonderful, flowery phrases as "the rented car was attacked by unknown villains who in a fit of frenzy, broke the window." It went on and on in a stream of flowery Italian language.

Finally, we initialed the document, satisfied that it was a reasonable explanation of what happened, and then we were able to leave and drive to Florence, get another car and get back to our rented home. I have to say, it took a long time to get it all done, but the police were courteous and well-meaning, even though the station captain gave our arresting officers a hard time, for some reason. So much for Arezzo.

Morris M. Weiss, M.D.

B. Cortona

Cortona is a classic hill town that, on a clear day, has a panoramic view across the Plain of Valdichiana to Lake Trasimeno. The town is located midway between Arrezo and Lake Trasimeno. This hill town dates back to the Villanovan occupation in the ninth century, evolving into an Etruscan center similar to our discussion of the twelve other major Etruscan centers scattered throughout Etruria. Park your car and wander the narrow winding streets that meander up and down the hillside. Try to find the Passeggiata—the walk from the Church of San Domenico to the public gardens, and enjoy the views across the Plain of Valdichiana at the base of the hill.

Make your way to the center of town (Piazza della Repubblica). Close by is the Palazzo Pretoria, containing—you guessed it—the Museo dell' Accademia Etrusca. The Etruscan collection has an excellent representation of classic black Bucchero ware and various bronze sculptures. These were retrieved from the three major tumuli and other smaller tombs in the plain below the hill, dating from the sixth through the fourth centuries B.C.

C. Perugia (Etrurian: Perusna; Latin: Perusia)

Perugia was one of the twelve Etruscan city states and previously a Villanovan settlement. The city flourished in the sixth century B.C.; what is left is a portion of the city wall and the famous arched city gate (Archo Etrusco or Arco di Augusto), found in the northeast corner of the modern city near the Palazzo Gallenga.

In the Palazzo Gallenga is the famous language summer school that foreign students attend in preparation for study in Italy. Here, in a few weeks, you can learn to speak Italian and take notes in the college-level courses, and even begin to think in Italian. This is a modern city with an industrial base, but also a university town in the medieval part of the city, within the old Etruscan and Roman walls.

The wealth and power of Perugia in the second and third centuries B.C. can be appreciated in the ancient wall and gates around the old city. Though built and rebuilt over the centuries, Etruscan wall segments remain. The two most important gates are the Arco di

Augusto and the Porta Marzia. The former is made up of an original upper portion and a lower portion built in various periods.

There are two levels of sculptured heads in relief. The first tier is three Etruscan deities in the upper register of the arch—more defined in later reliefs in a combination of Etruscan and Greek iconography. The Arco di Augusto is decorated with a frieze of shields and columns.

There are two major museums in Perugia. The Galleria Nazionale del Umbria contains Umbrian art from the Middle Ages and Renaissance periods. To see Etruscan objects, visit the Convent of San Dominico, which houses the state archives and the Museo Archeologia Nazionale del' Umbria. The Etruscan art is exhibited around the cloister and upstairs in the converted convent. Etruscan jewelry and mirrors are featured.

Also in this space is the Museo Prehistorico (Prehistoric Museum), with finds from the Monte Cetona, depicting Stone Age, Neolithic, and Iron Age material culture. I will discuss this further in the Monte Cetona section, since I spent a day studying the museum's Cetona collection and exploring the caves where the finds were discovered in 1928 and 1929.

After enjoying the narrow city streets and upper reaches of Perugia, descend to the Viale Roma, which exits the city in the southeast corner and travel about six kilometers (four miles) to the area of Etruscan cemeteries. The area is called the Ipogeo dei Volumnia. Hewn from living rock, and with a very elaborate architectural interior, the largest of the tombs represented the several generations of the Volumnian family. When it was discovered, this elaborate tomb, with arched ceilings resembling a roof with timber beams, and with several rooms, was filled with elaborate ash urns carved in high relief, containing the remains of this wealthy Perugian family and attesting to the prosperity of the city. This is the most famous example of the multitude of tombs found in the hills outside Perugia.

D. Lake Trasimeno (Lago Trasimeno) & Environs
Castiglione del Lago
Passignano sul Trasimeno

Lake Trasimene (or Trasimeno) is a picturesque, shallow body of water that deserves a brief giro. On the north shore is the quaint town of Passignano sul Trasimeno, with castle ruins and medieval walls. On the east side of the lake is Castiglione del Lago, a town built on a small peninsula jutting into the lake. Although the medieval ruins dominate your vision, the Etruscans did enjoy this site for fishing and swimming, and Etruscan finds have been excavated that were dedicated to a local god—a prepubertal boy. The city-state of Chuisi controlled this area.

South of the lake is Paciano, and southwest is the Citta' della Pieve—both very attractive Renaissance/Middle Ages towns worth a stop for a nice lunch. But alas, there are no Etruscan necropoli or small museos. Remember, if you are really reading this book, any building, town, necropolis, or museum displaying treasures after the second century B.C. is much too modern for your taste at this moment.

7

The West Coast

A west coast sojourn is a must if the Etruscans are to be fully understood and appreciated. The Tyrrhenian Sea, along the west coast of Italy, was the hub of Etruscan commercial activity over many centuries. Ships plying these waters traded with Greek colonies in the southern Italian peninsula, and the islands of Sicily, Elba, and Sardinia and their local Mediterranean venues. The Etruscan ships carried all manner of goods, but particularly metal ore of iron, copper, and tin from the Apennine Mountains.

Etruscan trade routes extended to the north African coast and east to the Greek isles and as far as Lydia (modern Turkey), Phoenicia (modern Lebanon and Israel), and Egypt, just to mention a few. History records several naval battles between the Etruscan fleet and rival Greek city states, especially Syracuse on the east coast of Sicily.

Of course, if you are touring Tuscany near Siena, a short drive west will put you in the vicinity of many Etruscan coastal tomb sites. However, most travelers prefer to stay in the romantic and scenic mid-Tuscan region. If you are in Pisa, visiting the Leaning Tower, a quick glance at the map locates you on the Arno, just before the river empties into the Mediterranean Sea.

All the sites discussed in this section lie due south of Pisa, almost to Rome. Again, heading south from Pisa is not the usual route taken by the meandering traveler. Often, it is east, back to Florence, or north to Milan.

Morris M. Weiss, M.D.

I recommend that your west coast excursion begin when you first deplane at Leonardo da Vinci Airport in Rome. Rome's airport lies west of the city, right on the coast. In fact, a portion of one of the major runways lies atop the silted-in harbor of Nero's navy. Instead of picking up your rental car after busing into Rome (don't ever pick up your car at the airport if you have never driven into Rome), get the rental car at the airport and head directly north to Cerveteri and Tarquinia. This will save you at least one day of hassle in negotiating Roman traffic and an expensive hotel room. Save Rome for the end of your trip.

The entry into Rome's center city from the north is easier to navigate from Highway A1, running down the center of the peninsula, than approaching from the east or west, unless your great-great-grandmother was a homing pigeon and you spoke Italian in another life. When you arrive at your hotel, the concierge will call the Rome rental car office and they will pick up your car. Use taxis or buses to move about Rome, and a taxi to the airport for your final flight home.

Remember—the highway planners of the cities of Europe were more humanistic than America's urban engineers, who destroyed our cities by bulldozing vast alleys of houses to make way for eight- to ten-lane expressways. Rome's expressways stop ten to fifteen miles from the center of town, and a maze of radial streets and piazzas leads you, with luck, to your hotel.

This modest inconvenience preserves the beauty and allure of hundreds of neighborhoods, best viewed from a taxi or bus, instead of trying to preserve your marriage with "You should have turned back there!" "I saw the same Roman temple ten minutes ago!" or "Turn left—the Pope doesn't live here!"

A. Cerveteri (Etruscan: Caistra Cisra; Latin: Caere)

Follow E80 (via Aurelia) to the north after you leave the airport. Cerveteri was one of the major Etruscan city states during the Archiac Period (575–480 B.C.) – at the height of the Etruscan power in this part of the world. The only reason to visit this small country town, 45 kilometers northwest of Rome, is to visit the Necropolis of the

Banditaccia—the cemetery of Cerveteri in the seventh and sixth centuries B.C.

When you enter Cerveteri, make your way to the Piazza Santa Maria, dominated by a twelfth century A.D. castle, built in part on old Etruscan walls. In the piazza is a small museum (Museo Nazionale Cerita) with a collection of Etruscan art found in the local tombs. However, the best material from the magnificent tombs in this area will be found in the Villa Gulia (the Etruscan Museum) in Rome (see Rome section).

The City of the Dead has a main street two kilometers long with many side streets. Tombs consist of tumuli (large, rounded mounds, usually covered with grass with a stone base—some as many as 30 meters in diameter); rock hewn tombs with several rooms; and cube tombs made up of tufa blocks that are similar to the Orvieto tombs. The cube tombs are all aboveground and appear as semi-detached condos. The tranquility and virtual silence of this City of the Dead is a good place to collect your thoughts.

Of the hundreds of tombs, a few are worth mentioning, including:

- Tumulo dei Capitelli
- Tomba dei Letti e Sarcofagi
- Tomba dei Vasi Greci
- Tomba dei Rilievi
- Tumulo della Quercia
- Tombei delle Spianta

Cerveteri was a wealthy metropolis; yet little is known about the ancient city. Only a small part of it has been systematically excavated. As most Etruscan sites, it lies on a tufa plateau.

The tombs have been studied by modern scholars and antiquarians, but for centuries they had been looted. The vases, sarcophagi, and other artifacts of daily living and warfare are scattered throughout the museums and private collections of the world.

For my own taste, the sarcophagus of a married couple, dated to the second half of the sixth century B.C., now resting peacefully in the Villa Gulia, is one of the great masterpieces of funerary art of any time or civilization. A similar sarcophagus, possibly by the same artist, is in the Louvre in Paris.

A final thought on Cerveteri: The Regolini-Galassi Tomb, in the Sorbo region of the Necropolis, produced masterpieces of Etruscan jewelry, now found in the Museo Gregoriano Etrusco—the Etruscan section of the vast Vatican Museum complex (see description of the Vatican Museum and how to reach this area). Cerveteri, Vulci, and Tarquinia, a short distance from the sea, had their own seaports that acted as emporiums for trading with the Mediterranean world. The emporium for Cerveteri was Pyrgi, or Santa Severa (modern Palo Laziale). There also was a harbor at Alsium, a bit south of Cerveteri, but we will confine our discussion to Pyrgi, just north of Cerveteri. The major autostrada A12, and the old historic Roman road Via Aurelia (E80), out of Rome, will take you to these sites.

B. Pyrgi

Pyrgi deserves a brief discussion, because here is a collection of shrines and temples reflecting the Greek, Carthagenian, and Etruscan cultures that came together at this trading center. At about the same time, Naukratis, in Egypt, was opened as a trading center in the now silted-in Canopic branch of the Nile, but in the seventh century B.C., it was open to shipping. I mention Naukratis because I had the privilege to excavate at this site with Professors Albert Leonard Jr., and the late William Coulson.

Excavations at Pyrgi unearthed three rectangular gold foil sheets, written in Etruscan and Phoenician. There was great excitement at first, because here, perhaps, was finally the Etruscan Rosetta Stone. The Phoenician was easily read, but the Etruscan inscription was not identical, so the Etruscan language remains indecipherable, even after exhaustive attempts of the best linguists working with archaeologists and philologists.

C. Tarquinia (Latin: Tarquinii)

Follow E80 (Via Aurelia) northward along the coast to Tarquinia, which today is a combination of medieval precincts with the requisite towers and a modern, rather dreary, somewhat dusty and shabby, small city of about thirteen thousand. As most Etruscan sites, ancient and contemporary Tarquinia lie on adjacent limestone (not tufa) plateaus, overlooking the Marta River, five kilometers inland from the Tyrrhenian Sea.

Probably the best way to orient yourself to the surrounding Etruscan tomb complex is to go immediately to the main square of Tarquinia (Piazza Cavour), where the Museo Nazionale Tarquiniense (National Tarquinian Museum) is located in the lovely Gothic palace (Palazzo Vitelleschi). The museum contains room after room of Etruscan treasures, gleaned from the many local tombs. Information on how best to negotiate and visit the tombs can be found in the museum. Etruscan Tarquinia is just to the east on another limestone ridge.

A few words are in order to appreciate the importance of a visit to this site. Although the aesthetics of the town and surrounding area are not up to the heart of Tuscany; nevertheless, Tarquinia is the cradle of Etruscan civilization and the leader at the apogee of her power.

Tarquinia was one of the twelve original city-states and the house of Tarquin, possibly the head of the Etruscan Confederation.

Virgil's account calls him Tarchon, either the brother or son of Tyrrhenius, who was the son of Atys, the ruler of Lydia far to the east (modern Turkey). During a famine, Atys sent Tyrrhenius, along with citizens of Lydia, to start life anew in the west.

Here, along the coast of Etruria, Tarquinia was founded. Here also, Demaratus of Corinth, in the eighth century B.C., settled, and his son, Lucinus Tarquinius Priscus, became the fifth king of Rome. And here also, from a farmer's plowed furrow, sprang Tages, who taught the Etruscans the art of divination, which was passed on to the Romans.

The skill of divination included predictions from lightning, birds, and inspection of animal livers.

The professional Auger (priest-like figure), who is a specialist in liver interpretation, became an integral part of Roman life. The Roman concept of Genius is the part of each individual (his double) who came into being to guide his destiny and his life's journey, including his health. Before settling in a new area, the Romans examined the liver of local animals. If the organ was diseased, it meant the area was unhealthful. The animal was sacrificed to ascertain if the Genius of the local deity looked favorably on the new building site.

In this indirect way, the Etruscan concept of Genius and divination that began with Tages in Tarquinia permeated public health concepts and the decisions of Roman planners. The Etruscans had the earliest effect on public health concepts.

Visiting the painted tombs of Tarquinia is a must if you desire to understand Etruscan life and culture. These are the best preserved painted tombs in all Etruria because of the properties of the paint and the surface preparation techniques used by the Tarquins. The intensity and range of different colors after twenty-six hundred years never ceases to amaze me. The residual feelings and impression left on my cerebral cortex is of an aristocracy and citizenry filled with a life of sport, dance, music, and banqueting and a superstitious fear of their gods and the afterlife.

The tombs are in four groups, so a good way to systematically attack the idea of seeing enough of the tombs to obtain a feel for how the sixth century B.C. Etruscan lived and died is to systematically look at these four areas. I say "sixth century B.C." because the majority of the best painted tombs are from this era, in the so-called Archaic Period. In the necropolis surrounding Tarquinia are at least six thousand tombs, with two or three hundred painted tombs of the wealthy citizens. I will include a list of significant tombs that is far from complete. Remember, tombs constantly require repair in an attempt to preserve the painted walls.

Over the years, tourists have introduced bacteria from their skin and respiratory tracts that thrive in the damp clime of the tombs. The Italian government is preserving the best paintings by air conditioning the chambers, controlling the humidity, and putting Plexiglas shields on the wall over the painted surfaces.

Don't be disappointed if the tomb you want to see is not open the day you arrive. This sepulcher may be arbitrarily closed by the guards, or under repair. Some of the tombs are reserved for scholars and special tours. If a specialist guide is available, and of course, for the proper recompense, keys suddenly appear that open locks to chambers for special viewing. This is true, of course, the world over. In my experience, this strategy is most useful in the Valley of the Kings in Egypt, to penetrate the depths of often-closed pharaonic resting places.

I am indebted to the Alta Macadam, editor of the *Blue Guide of Northern Italy, from the Alps to Rome*, for the suggestion of geographically breaking up this huge necropolis of over 6,000 tombs into four areas.

The first is outside the Tarquinian Gate, the second near the modern cemetery, the third a small collection of tombs one-half kilometer further down the cemetery road, and the last group a bit further down the road. The *Blue Book Guide* lists several tombs in each of these four areas; all are worth visiting and have merit in their own right.

Sybille Haynes is the author of *Etruscan Civilization, A Cultural History*—a recent noteworthy addition to Etruscan literature. This tome should be required reading before you undertake a trip to Etruria to mingle amongst the rocks and ruins of the Etruscans. Even if your interest is piqued by the Etruscans, and you are destined to become an armchair Etruscologist, begin with Haynes and then work backward with earlier writers.

My favorites are included in the bibliography at the end of this book. These titles cohabit with several hundred other Etruscan monographs and excavation reports on my overstuffed library shelves.

The following list of the tombs Sybille Haynes describes in her book, and a study of these tombs, will give the interested traveler an excellent overview of the 6,000 tombs Tarquinia has to offer. I have unabashedly lifted these from her chapter on Tarquinia.

- Tomb of the Augurs (Tomba degli Auguri)
- Tomb of the Cock (Tomba del Gallo)

- Tomb of the Olympic Games (Tomba delle Olimpiadi)
- Tomb of the Bigas (Tomba delle Bighe)
- Tomb of the Barron (Tomba delle Barone)
- Cardarelli Tomb (Tomba Cardarelli)
- Tomb of the Lionesses (Tomba delle Leonesse)
- Tomb of Hunting and Fishing (Tomba della Caccia e Pesca)
- Tomb of the Juggler (Tomba de Giocolieri)
- Tomb of the Triclinium (Tomba del Triclinio)

We will finish our stopover at Tarquinia with two side trips, if there is time in your schedule. Follow the road out of the necropolis to the Monte Romono Road; then look to your left for the remains of an aqueduct (total distance, about 8 to 10 kilometers). Watch for the Acropolis of Tarquinia sign. About a one kilometer walk will bring you to the great altar ruins (Ara della Regina).

This platform was built of ashlar blocks in the fourth century B.C., but appears to be a religious site lost in the mists of prehistory.

The pride and joy of the Museo Nazionale Archaeologio, in the main piazza previously described, is a pair of high-relief winged horses from the pediment of the Temple Ruth of the fourth century B.C. structure that sat atop this great platform. The horses are a masterpiece of Etruscan sculpture that originally included a biga (horses and chariot).

Tarquinia's port was called Garvisca, and here an international trade emporium existed, similar to Cerveteri's port of Pyrgi, discussed earlier. When the Romans conquered Tarquinia in the third century B.C., they built Porto Clementino, which survived for 1500 years—but now the area is a sand beach and barren salt flats.

D. Vetulonia (Etrurian: Vetluna)

As we proceed north along E80 (Via Aurelia or Via Etrusca, depending on what map you have unfolded in your lap), the next major site is Vetulonia. Find Grossetto on your map; then just to the northwest, on a ridge near the sea, is Vetulonia. The ridge was the home of a Villanovan early Iron Age village before morphing into a wealthy Etruscan city-state.

Vetulonia was an important member of the Etruscan confederation during the flowering of Etruscan culture in the seventh century B.C. The site today seems quite a distance from the sea, but early on, the inhabitants could look down on a shoreline and a shallow lagoon bustling with ships and commerce. This shallow gulf gradually silted in; by Roman times, it was a salty marsh, and later, a mosquito-infested fresh water lake. In the modern era, the lake was drained, producing fertile farmland and eliminating the mosquito—and thus malaria—allowing the human population to return safely to this area. Now the sea is further to the west.

The Etruscan/Roman port was probably present-day Castigliona della Pescaia, slightly southwest of the ridge. There are remnants of early city walls from the fifth century B.C. that were originally about 5 kilometers in circumference. Vetulonia is surrounded by necropoli that produced many artifacts of local manufacture, and imported pieces from places as distant as Egypt and Phoenica. The hills around Vetulonia were rich in copper mines, and the wealthy merchant families of the seventh century B.C. (before the walls mentioned above) imported art treasures from the people with whom they did business, attesting to the wide-ranging trading networks of the ports along the west coast of Etruria. The artifacts include many well-turned and painted terra cotta vases, plus bronze, silver, and gold objects. Many of these were moved to the Etruscan Museum in Florence and Orvieto.

The tombs themselves are often trench-like and lined with stone slabs. The seventh century burials are the richest because, in all likelihood, Vetulonia began to lose her prominence when the harbor began to silt up. The Tumulo della Pietera and the Tumulo del Diavolina, about 3 kilometers from the ridge ruins, are worth a visit. A local guide is recommended. The classic Roman symbols of the fasces (bundle of sticks), curial chair, and toga are said to originate in Vetulonia.

E. Populonia (Etrurian: Fufluna; Latin: Pupluna)

Our final stop along the coast will be Populonia. For the Etruscans, Pisa, north of Populonia and near the mouth of the Arno River, was probably the northern end of their immediate territory. For me, Pisa belongs to Florence and Fiesole. These three sites are so identified with the Italian Renaissance that we often see them together when doing our "Grand Tour."

Pisa is discussed with San Gimignano and Volterra.

Populonia was perched on a promontory, preceded by an early Iron Age village. The early real estate agents always found the best views in salubrious climates, and Populonia certainly meets these criteria. On a clear day, the islands of Elba and even Corsica can be seen.

The port Baratti, on the south side of the Gulf of Baratti, made Populonia an important trading center in ancient Etruria. Again, these hills were filled with iron, tin, and copper. Smelting furnaces have been identified and the eighth to sixth century Etruscans traded for perfumes and other precious artifacts as far away as Greece and Syria, as well as the previously mentioned Egypt and Phoenicia.

A small private museum (Museo Archaelogia Gasparri) has a small collection of terra cotta and bronze artifacts, but the really good material is in Florence.

Populonia is another of the Etruscan city-states that flourished during the Archaic Period (sixth and fifth centuries B.C.). Her wealth was from the metals in the hills, and the smelting furnaces probably processed the iron ore from nearby Elba. During the intermediate period (fifth to fourth centuries B.C.), she maintained a prominent position.

The ubiquitous Etruscan cemetery is, of course, present for our viewing. In the sixth century B.C., a house-shaped tomb—with a pitched roof and the roof ridge adorned with various terra cotta and stone antefixes and acroteria, not unlike the cowboy hat roof decorations from Murlo—made an appearance. The great wealth of the oligarchy built tombs in several areas, including the necropoli of San Cerbone Casone and Poggi della Porcareccia. The Tomb of the Chariots (Tomba dei Carri) and the Tomb of the Bronze Fans (Tomba dei Flabelli di Bronzo) have produced treasures beyond the discussion of this volume, but a visit to the empty tombs is worthwhile.

As always, a local guide, to save time and to see the best tombs, is recommended.

8

Central

A. Lake Bolsena

For the past several years, Lake Bolsena and its environs have attracted my attention. In an unidentified site, somewhere between Orvieto and nearby Lake Bolsena (southwest of Orvieto), buried just beneath the surface, is where the Etruscan League assembled annually for religious celebration and political and business consulting and discussion. About all we know of this important event comes from brief comments by the Roman writer Livy. Kings of the twelve Etruscan city-states elected one of their group to preside over the annual event, and a head priest might have been elected, since the Etruscan cities were bound together by a common religion, and not a formal political or military alliance. This event, called the "Phantom Voltumnae," probably had athletic contests as well—perhaps in the Olympic tradition that had been flourishing in Greece for two to three centuries before this convention in the fifth and fourth centuries B.C.

The saying "all roads lead to Rome" must have existed for the Etruscans as well—namely, all roads led to the famous "Phantom Voltumnae" on Lake Bolsena, surely a resort town for many millennia. But where are the roads that converged on this area? I have, for several years, pored over maps, both ancient and contemporary, to see if the modern roads are simply superimposed on ancient byways. For me, this has been a task that, simply put, has been unrewarding, since my simple technique cannot decide if there is a network of old roads that would necessarily lead to the site of what must have been a colorful gathering of serious religious and political discussion—but also a great business fair, with a midway filled with hucksters, gamblers, and petty thieves.

My enthusiasm was waning until I read a wonderful article about the discovery of early Bronze Age roadways in the agricultural system of Mesopotamia in northeast Syria, using the study of declassified photographs from the spy satellite Corona program. The area surveyed was free of cities and villages, so much information was soon obtained and verified on the ground. The French satellite systems SPOT and LANDSTAT, with low resolution, were checked, but are not refined enough for archaeological research.

Next, I checked sources in America. Penetrating the bureaucracy of the EROS Data Center in Sioux Falls, South Dakota, and NASA images in Los Angeles proved difficult. I was looking at this area during the 9-11-2001 terrorist attacks, so a letter and phone call from an obscure cardiologist in Louisville, Kentucky, didn't get past the initial screening process. The New York Public Library, to its credit, answered my request, but its extensive map collection did not contain the Italian maps needed for the Lake Bolsena region. There is a web site linking Italian university libraries, but this turned out to be too difficult to navigate for my simple computer mind. My last stab was to the NASA Global Hydrology and Climate Center in Huntsville, Alabama. Alas, no response to my ardent entreaty.

So on my most recent trip to Etruria, I trundled over to the east shore of Lake Bolsena (Greenwich coordinates North 42.5° by East 120°) and began a giro around the lake, to survey the terrain with my own eyes. As others who have made this pilgrimage have surmised, nothing is discernible, because modern Bolsena and surrounding villages carpet most of the area that is fruitful for archaeology research. Some day, more powerful subsurface radar images will be declassified and this site will be located. In the meantime, any structures scheduled for rebuilding, or repaving of old roads, should have their substructures examined for Etruscan building foundations and remnants of ancient roadbeds.

What of modern Bolsena? This area is certainly worth a brief visit to survey a quiet, middle-class Italian resort town, free of ogling and elbowing tourists. I particularly liked the open-air market—filled with low-price domestic clothing and household items, side by side with pirated music CDs, radios, stereos, and sports equipment. There also are low-price seafood and pizza restaurants.

Geographically, Lake Bolsena is in the center of Etruria, but because of major roads like the A1 Autostrada, Bolsena has gradually atrophied. Along her shores and in the surrounding hills, and even on her lake bottom, will be found Etruscan treasures. In this vicinity is the best chance of finding the Etruscan Rosetta stone that will finally decipher the structure of the language carved in Greek letters, borrowed from their Greek neighbors just to the south around the Bay of Naples.

Bolsena was founded on the west side of the lake by the inhabitants of Etruscan Orvieto (the Volsinii), who were displaced when the Roman army decimated their city in 280 B.C. Today, the town is nondescript. It can be seen best with a view of Lake Bolsena as you approach the area from the top of the last hill (which is actually the edge of the ancient volcano) before you descend to the lake on the Viterbo-Siena Road. Bolsena today is best remembered by a thirteenth century miracle, when a Bohemian priest was convinced the drop of blood on the altar linen was from the Host.

The lake is the largest and most northern of the three volcanic lakes in the northern province of Lazio, just to the east of the edge of Tuscany. The shores of the lake are lined with small trees that create a rather limpid light. The lake, with its two small islands, has a rather forlorn look, but archaeological evidence shows continuous habitation since prehistoric times (good fishing with an abundant supply of eels). The ancient necropoli (Poggio, Pesce, Varano, Vietana, and Sula) are featured in this area, but the valuable artifacts can only be found in the National Archaeology Museum in Florence and the Villa Gulia in Rome.

B. Orvieto (Ancient Volsinii)

Before I pen this chapter, I must confess that I own a prejudice about Orvieto. This love comes from great memories of travel with my wife, food, wine, and, of course, Etruscan ruins.

The memory is still vivid of our honeymoon stay at the Hotel Maatani on Via Maatani, with our room on the second floor sticking out from the hotel like a giant proboscis. We had a frontal view of the magnificent Duomo with its horizontal, alternating gray basalt and white marble walls. This monumental Gothic temple to God is one of the most beautiful in all of Europe. The Duomo sits on top of the plateau and is surrounded by smaller buildings and palaces, giving additional authority to its beauty.

But I get ahead of myself. Let's go back in the shallow, broad Paglia Valley in Umbria, where sits the tufa mesa of Orvieto. As you approach Orvieto, this huge rock suddenly appears. There are no surrounding hills or other mountains, so the effect is very dramatic. The mound reminds me of the classic Italian Christmas cake, Il Gran Pandoro, in contour. Orvieto is one of the original twelve Etruscan city-states, and the height of its power came in the fourth to the second centuries B.C. However, human occupation can be traced to the early Iron Age villages of the Villanovans (tenth to eighth centuries B.C.). The Villanovans (pre-Etruscan inhabitants of this area) always used the plateaus of volcanic tufan rocky hills to establish their primitive mud and wattle huts, villages, and eventually, cities.

Approaching Orvieto from the south gives a view of the city, and you can ascend slowly to the top, enjoying the architecture of the past five hundred years in her houses and churches. Even more important, the southern entrance has the best Etruscan tombs, found just a few yards from the road. If you approach from the north, where the modern train station is found, at the base of the hill is the Orvieto Scalo (Little Funicolare), which will give you a ride on a cable car up to the oldest part of the city. You will learn and enjoy so much more taking the winding road to the top, but many are not able to pass up the thrill of a sky ride in the Funicolare.

Entering from the south requires an obligatory visit to the necropoli (burial sites). These are not small cave tombs carved into the tufa, but rectangular houses of the dead—built of tufa blocks and about six feet tall inside. The rooms are about 8 x 8 x 6, on average. The tombs are laid out like homes along a street—carefully constructed in a perfect grid. The street is two feet above the floor of the tomb, so watch carefully when you step inside, or you will bump and scrape your head on the lintel above the entering space. This can create a small scab on a bald pate such as mine.

The lintel was the top of a door that led to the house of the dead. On the lintel is carved in Etruscan letters (using the Greek alphabet) the name of the deceased. This is a favorite Etruscan site of mine, since you can see how meticulous they were in creating an afterlife, with a setting similar to their own living condition. This particular cemetery has several streets filled with tombs, and the archaeologists continue to uncover more each year. The street of tombs ends at the vertical tufa wall that rises 560 meters to Orvieto. After spending some time absorbing the ambiance of this setting, and in the summer enjoying the many wildflowers growing in virtually every nook and cranny, the coolness and shade of the tombs can be a relief from a high, warm August Etruscan sun.

Get back in your car and enjoy the winding ascent to the piazza at the top that contains the Duomo. Every neighborhood and street of importance radiates from the piazza. About halfway up to the summit, on a small ledge beside the road, are the remnants of a typical Etruscan temple (Temple of Belvedere) with the internal walls (alae) producing three rooms, or cellas. The rooms open onto a broad patio-like area in the front of the temple. As with all Etruscan buildings, only the stone foundations remain, with scattered roof tiles. The walls were constructed of mud, wattle, and plaster, with wooden pillars holding up the roof.

Orvieto (Volsinii) history is tragic and rather convoluted. The pre-Etruscan inhabitants, or Villanovans, have left only a few hints of their existence. We know from Roman annals that Volsinii's rulers and aristocrats had many slaves. In the period 295-280 B.C., the slaves revolted and their masters, soft from a life of luxury, were overwhelmed. The aristocracy begged the Romans to intercede in its behalf. The Romans had been slowly picking off the Etruscan city-states over the past century or two, and Volsinii was a prize they wanted and needed. The city was strategically located as a commercial center, with many roads leading to and from Volsinii. The Roman army destroyed Orvieto (Volsinii), essentially razing it to the ground, and many families were displaced to the edge of nearby Lake Bolsena, where they began life again on a new city site. The new and old Volsinii never recovered enough to reestablish her influence in this area.

After reaching the Duomo, take time to smell the roses. First, visit the Duomo and marvel at the works of art adorning the interior. All guide books will lead you from chapel to chapel, and list all the "masterpieces" for you to savor and digest, and will not be repeated. Face the Duomo's front door and look directly across the piazza to your left. There is a small, narrow street that begins to descend from the summit. A few yards down the street on the left is Maurizio's, a wonderful restaurant with Maurizio's own Chianti label. Eat slowly and enjoy a few carafes of his vino. There are, of course, many other good places to wine and dine atop Orvieto.

Take time to find portions of the great fortress walls that remain from the time Orvieto was a walled city (thirteenth to fifteenth centuries A.D.). The brick work is impressive and the view of the Paglia Valley, with its cultivated fields, vineyards and olive orchards, often in a misty haze in the early morning and late afternoon, has no rival. The fortress wall is built directly into the sheer sides of the tufa, and produces an interesting bond of nature and man's ingenuity. This bonding wall is seen clearly as you ascend in the car. Capturing Orvieto from the outside must have been nearly impossible, so her capture from inside was probably the reason she could be defeated.

9

The South

A. Etruscan Rome

For centuries, every scholar, both major and minor, has brought forth his or her pet theories as to why a small group of Etruscan, Latin, and Sabine settlements (Iron Age) in the lower Tiber Valley became the great city we call Rome ("The Eternal City," or more to my liking, "Caput Mundi"—"Head of the World").

I believe, first of all, that geography dictated the site. The political and commercial control of the Italian peninsula was possible from this "mid-boot" site, with an easy ford of the Tiber at the Isola Tevere (island). Far enough inland from the mouth of the Tiber, which empties into the Tyrrhenian Sea, the city could avoid pirates and naval incursions, and is the central focal point for the movement of armies and trading of goods, of every imaginable type, from north to south.

Why and how the Roman people had the energy to develop their empire, and the reason why the city became the focal point of Christendom and the Roman Catholic Church, is for scholars more insightful than myself. But for purposes of this piece of travel literature, the siting of Rome on the Tiber banks was, in the modern vernacular, "a no-brainer." Here, Etruscan nobleman from Tarquinia and other powerful city-states came to protect their southern flank and control the passage of goods from their Greek city-state neighbors just to the south, around the Bay of Naples, and as far south as the tip of the boot, in Apulia.

The Romans date the founding of their city to 21 April, 753 B.C. – a remarkably specific date. Legend has it that Romulus (origin of the city's name) and his twin brother Remus, suckled by a she-wolf, established an Iron Age village on the Palantine Hill and later on the Capitaline Hill. The latter was probably a religious and political center. Archaeologists have found evidence of rude huts dating to this legendary prehistoric era.

On these two hills, and surely on the other five major hills of Rome, Etruscan kings ruled until 510 B.C., when they were overthrown by Roman citizens and the Republic was born.

The Etruscans came to Rome as builders. They laid out a formal city and drained the swamps. They were craftsman, builders, politicians, religious figures, and probably doctors. They were city people, and not rural folk, who had inhabited Rome from the ninth to the seventh centuries B.C.

Just to burden you with a bit more Etruscan/Roman history, we should mention that the early kings of Rome were Etruscans. King Servius Tullius developed a census system, a new taxation system, military service, and divided the populace into tribes according to wealth. Lucius Tarquinius Superbus was the last Etruscan king of Rome. He was a tyrannical monarch and he was expelled by the Roman populace; then begins the classic Roman Republic. For several centuries, many Roman Republic consuls—the high political figures—had Etruscan names.

It is of interest that the Tarquin royal family allowed the royal ladies to ride in the carriages in Rome, where only the Roman Vestal Virgins, unaccompanied by a male, were allowed in the carriage. Women who were true Roman citizens were rarely seen in public in Rome, unless under the most unusual of circumstances.

The Etruscan influence continued long after Rome began to take on and pick off the Etruscan states in the fourth century B.C. The emperor Augustus entrusted the education of his grandson to an antiquarian and Etruscologist Verrus Flaccus, and made Gaius Maecenas, the son of an ancient Etruscan family, his confidant. In fact, Augustus's tomb resembles early Etruscan architecture. The

The Mystery of the Tuscan Hills

emperor Claudius married into a noble Etruscan Cerveterian family. It was the emperor Claudius who wrote the twenty-volume history of the Etruscans—unfortunately lost to us.

This introduction to the Etruscan influence on the early history of Rome hopefully will help the traveler locate in his mind a starting point—if you are crazy enough to search out the Etruscans in Rome, as I have tried to do. This is a formidable task, unless you are pointed in the proper direction.

Also, trying to stay focused on Etruscan Rome is almost impossible, when your senses are overwhelmed with the Rome that is above ground—that is, trying to sort out Roman Rome, Renaissance Rome, Baroque Rome, Catholic Rome, and modern Rome, all cobbled together. Often in a one- or two-block area, all these are visible and usually of historical and architectural significance.

So where to start? My recommendation is to go to the Trastevere section, along the Tiber, and ask your taxi driver to drop you off at the Tiber Island. The Ponte Cesto is the oldest extant Roman bridge (46 B.C.) and will lead you from the street onto the Tiber Island. This island is incredibly important to Roman history because from 295 to 293 B.C., Rome suffered from a great plague. The Roman priests tried every known intervention, all with no effect.

Finally, they were advised to go to the Oracle at Delphi in Greece. She sent them to Epidauros to obtain a snake from the Temple of Aesklepios. This was brought back to Rome and, just before the ship docked, the snake jumped off the ship's deck and swam to the Tiber Island. The plague suddenly abated. The Romans surrounded the edges of the island with travertine marble, creating a shape similar to the ship. On the south end, an Aescalapian healing center was built. Now, there is a modern hospital called the Hospital Fatebenefratelli, on the north end of the island, and on the south end, the Church of San Bartolomeo, that was built over the ruins of the Aesklepian site.

This particular monument in Rome is of great interest to me, because of my writing in ancient medicine and an attempt to save a relief of the bust of Aesklepios carved into the travertine. It is a site worth visiting, and, if you are interested in the Etruscans, you are also in the right place.

Stand on the tip of the island and look down the river to see on the left side the entrance to a large, sewer-like object that is emptying into the Tiber. This is the Cloaca Maximus—the ancient drainage ditch built originally by the Etruscans. We will come back to that in a minute.

Just off to your east are the Palantine and Capitaline Hill and the Roman Forum. Now you must close your eyes and envision the Tiber River as a slowly flowing summer river—not overflowing the banks with the spring or fall floods, but moving from north to south, coming out of the Appenine hills and mountains, with thousands of small streams emptying into the river as it makes its way to the Tyrrhenian (Mediterranean) Sea.

Now imagine the Tiber without its stone walls, which are now the sides, so it looks more like a canal than a river, and imagine the streets being fifteen to twenty feet lower because, after two and a half millennia, the debris has raised the level of the city about two stories high. You must envision the area of the Forum at river level. Also, before the Roman Empire made the Forum into one of the most magnificent public areas the world has ever seen, this was open farmland.

The Iron Age settlers who lived atop the hill came down to the river to water their cattle and feed them in the grasslands. In ancient times, much of this was swamp. But the Etruscans cleared the swamps by digging this great ditch, which eventually became the covered sewer Cloaca Maximus.

The Cloaca Maximus not only drained the swamps, but controlled malaria, which was the curse of that part of the world. Originally, this was an open water course, later canalized, draining from northeast down to the Tiber by way of the Roman Forum. Tradition ascribed its development to Tarquinius Superbus. The original canal has been long covered, but some of the branch drains of the fifth century B.C. do exist, and the sewer that one sees now dates to 200 B.C. and was last rebuilt in 33 B.C. by Agrippa.

By draining this swampland, the Forum was developed; eventually, this was the busiest part of the city center. If you are able mentally to erase all of modern Rome that you see before you, it is possible to picture the city at the Tiber Island at the time of the original Etruscan habitation of this area.

Up on the Palatine hill, short sections of the earliest walls of Rome can be found. They are of Etruscan style, and it is unknown whether they were built by Etruscans, or the Romans copied the Etruscan method of building. But clearly, they are quite ancient. Also on the Palatine hill, shards of Etruscan pottery with Etruscan writing on several vessels have been found.

In the Forum Boarium (cattle market), the oldest market of ancient Rome, have been found Etruscan ruins and evidence of a classic three-celled Etruscan temple. Again, the Forum Boarium has many churches and fountains and ancient Roman temples, and is near the great building of the Teatro di Marcello on the Lungo Tevrere Aventino—the avenue that runs along the Tiber River in this district.

It is here, between the Tiber Island and back to the east to the Palatine hill, that one must imagine the Etruscan Rome. There is a famous church named Sant' Ombono, near the Teatro di Marcello. Underneath this building, and in surrounding space, archaeologists have found archaic Roman temples and Bronze and Iron Age shards, with traces of hut dwelling dating to the ninth and eighth centuries B.C.—that is, the Etruscan period and before.

We will now finish our survey of Etruscan Rome by visiting two great museums filled with the best Etruscan treasures. The Vatican Museum, which is really a series of many museums, has, on the far reaches of the second floor, the Etruscan museum. You arrive at this area by going through the Galley of Candelabras and the Galley of Tapestries. They end in the Vase Room, which is the beginning of the Etruscan exhibit: the Museo Gregorian Etrusco, founded in 1837 by Pope Gregory the XVI. Most of the contents are from southern Tuscany.

The Greek vases, found in abundance in Etruscan tombs, are impressive. There are twelve rooms filled with the best of Etruscan art. For my taste, the sarcophagi in room I and the gold jewelry in room II, from the Regolini-Galassi tomb found in 1836 near Caere, are breathtakers. The other rooms, II through XIIA and B, all contain treasures. This mini-tour ends in room XIV–XVIII, filled with Greek Italic and Etruscan vases.

For details of each room, I recommend the Blue Guide of Rome and environs. The Blue Guides are my favorite books for this type of "museuming," and there is no need for audio guides that, for my soul, take away much of the aesthetic pleasure of viewing a museum gallery.

One needs to take the Vatican Museum small parts at a time, if you have the luxury. Entering and taking either the long or short tour, and universally ending up in the Sistine Chapel, you simply overdose on the extravagance of art covering every wall, floor, and ceiling.

To end our Etruscan visit to Rome, see the Villa Gulia, in the northeast corner of the Borghese Gardens—upriver, north from the Vatican, but on the opposite side of the river. The Villa Gulia (complete name is Villa di Papa Gulia) was built between 1550 and 1555 for Pope Julian III. On a hot summer day, the Pope and his entourage rode upstream to "get away" from the steaming city and relax in his villa or in the Nymphaeum, found at the end of his elaborate gardens.

Today the Gardens are maintained, and on the right of the courtyard is a reproduction of an Etruscan temple (Temple Aletrium or Altari). The museum treasures are displayed in an uncluttered way and well-lit, as compared to the Etruscan section of the Archaeology Museum in Florence. Take your time and enjoy the vases of Greek and Etruscan origin. The aristocracy and oligarchs filled their tombs with the best of Attic and Corinthian ceramic vessels—imported from the Greek city-states over several centuries.

The best vase painters are well represented, and profited from this lucrative trade. Etruscan potters and vase painters also were quite skilled, although they never achieved in our modern eyes the aesthetic level reached by the best Greek potters and vase painters. Nevertheless, the indigenous artists were quite accomplished in their own right.

Don't miss, in room I, several cases containing Villanovan material (pre-Etruscan). The Villanovans lived primarily in the northern part of Tuscany and off to the northeast near Bologna. Terra cotta model huts, military equipment, and small statuary are to be enjoyed; they also teach us how the Villanovans lived, dressed, and made war. Make your way around the building with about thirty-four rooms. The full range of Etruscan bronzes, gold jewelry, and the sarcophagi, with husband and wife reposing on the lid for all eternity, will surely delight your senses.

When you're near the center of the wings, look out the windows and enjoy the courtyard with its portico, the Loggia, leading down the handsome stairs to the Nymphaeum—all enclosed within the formal garden. In the southeast corner is the Temple of Altari, a reproduction of exquisite accuracy and painted in the many colors used by ancient architects. We are used to our classical buildings as white marble, but all Greek and Roman public and religious structures were brightly painted.

This survey of Etruscan Rome can be accomplished in two days if you arise early and go back after lunch. Remember, the early bird gets the advantage at the Vatican Museum, where every tourist and student seems to congregate, waiting for the doors to open. If it is July or August and you don't have an unlimited amount of time, a few euros are well spent on a Vatican guide; this gets you to the front of the line, so you may avoid the hot, humid clime, even on an early Roman morning.

10

Return to the Core—Finale

A. Sarteano

I saved this section of my attempt at an Etruscan travel book, and penned it at the very last moment. Clearly for me, it is the most difficult section to write, and not for lack of information or desire.

The hurdle and hazard was to study this area to better envision Etruscan society. In the introduction of this monograph, I discussed the fact that most of what we know about Etruscan civilization comes from the tombs of prominent families, and from unearthing their major cities.

We understand fairly well the oligarchs. These families bred the merchant princes who produced the wealth and resulting political and military power. Some sons became generals, and the others ruler-priests (lucumones). We know of their banquets, sporting life, and refined clothing from the tomb-wall paintings, which we have looked at and discussed in this book.

But what of the common people (free and slave), who made up probably 95 percent or more of the entire population? What did they eat? What did they wear? What type of housing did they have? Detailed answers to these queries are impossible to find, but in my meandering in this region, I began to get a sense of what life must have been like.

I begin with Sarteano, once an Etruscan settlement. My family got to know this small, quiet town intimately during our month in the nearby rented farmhouse. Frequent visits to the local small family merchants for the necessities of daily living provided an understanding of the rhythm of life in a small hill town.

First of all, the natives have clearly preserved their relative quiet and pace of life. The narrow medieval gateway that once was the entrance into a walled lower city still stands. This portal is wide enough to allow two horses abreast, or now two bicycles or motorcycles, but only one automobile at a time. Everyone must stop, and then two or three cars at a time pass in, and then two or three cars pass out, with a briefly timed light—no roaring through town allowed.

Most of the medieval fortress wall is intact. As soon as you ascend a few stairs and a short ramped street, the area widens out into a small piazza. Narrow streets and alleys go at many angles, forming a 180-degree arc, or semicircle. As you slowly ascend to the crest of the hill crowned by an ancient nunnery (now a first-rate restaurant), the architecture unfolds. In the summer, dinner is alfresco in the restaurant. While awaiting your food, you can take a short flight of stairs to the top of the wall and enjoy the panorama of the valley below and the hills beyond—a checkerboard of tilled fields, vineyards, and olive orchards.

After a few visits, the rhythm of village life is very apparent and, with a bit of imagination, the traveler can carry himself back to the middle ages and beyond—to Etruscan and Villanovan life. Retail shops, houses, schools, restaurants, churches, and small manufacturing businesses are all interlaced and intertwined into an organic whole. All the necessities and staples of life are just a few yards away from every family.

The diet is traditional and has repeated itself for centuries. We in America are so used to eating foods of many different cultures and nationalities. In Sarteano, everything is fresh and purchased daily, with little need for refrigeration. All the food is "comfort" food.

A small museum (Museo Civico Archaelogico) in the Palazzo Gabrielli celebrates items from the warren of Etruscan tombs in the area around Sarteano. Cinerary urns, bronzes, and vases are nicely displayed.

One weekend, we witnessed a medieval fair in the piazza. Children and young adults in vintage costumes danced and entertained. The town was gussied up, and the shops were all open, selling souvenirs, lace, ceramics, clothing, and just about anything else you might need or thought you needed.

In the piazza were magicians, fortune tellers, blacksmiths, calligraphers, and food vendors, organized like our county fairs. I was entranced by a falconer who held several raptors, including an owl, on a stand and on his arm. His prized peregrine would fly from his hand and circle about, waiting for him to spin in a great circle a leather thong with a piece of meat, which the bird would dive down and devour. On one flight, the bird did not return and the falconer was frantic, until he realized his raptor was munching down on a live, plump pigeon on a nearly roof. So much for Sarteano: a picture of village life since time immemorial.

B. Cetona/Monte Cetona

Cetona is a must stop for prehistoric buffs. The village of Cetona is inviting, with the main street lined on both sides with handsome, well-cared-for buildings—some centuries old. The village Civic Center has all the information necessary to explain the town and local information.

Cetona and its environs includes Monte Cetona. After strolling about the main street, walk past the tower at the far end of the piazza and follow the street to Museo Civico per la Prehistoria del Monte Cetona (Civic Museum for the Prehistory of Monte Cetona). Buy a ticket and enjoy the display of the stone tools and dioramas of Stone and Bronze Age life, depicting the discoveries in the local caves. These were untouched deposits, and this is the most valuable Bronze Age site in all of Italy. There is, of course, a small Etruscan collection.

The stub of your ticket admits you to the Belverde Archaeologica Park, six kilometers from Cetona. Take the road back towards Sarteano. Follow the road signs and you soon are in front of a small administration building, resembling a state park building anywhere in the world. Every thirty to sixty minutes, a guided tour will lead you through the grottoes and caves at this most scenic and restful site.

The Mystery of the Tuscan Hills

The drive from Cetona to Monte Cetona must be done slowly, so as not to miss the low, soft hills; gently curving roads; trees and green hillsides; wildflowers and undulating fields in the shallow valleys between the hills. (If you are a cyclist, this is a spectacular day trip.) This short drive and exploration of the natural caves and hidden grottoes produced by huge travertine boulders that fell off Mount Cetona explains why there is evidence here of Neanderthal man (minimum 25,000 B.C. and, in this area, probably 30,000 to 35,000 B.C.), Stone Age cave dwellers, and Bronze Age clans. Plenty of water, caves for safety in inclement weather, and forested areas for hunting deer and boar, made this a paradise no civilization has turned down, including the Etruscans.

At the base of Mount Cetona is found a Bronze Age village with only stone foundations remaining, and a large boulder that crushed several houses is still in place.

C. Radicofani

In this same area, and actually closer to Sarteano, is a wedding-cake-shaped hill with a ruined castle atop, instead of the bride and groom. The castle reminds me of the castle at the end of Main Street at Disney World. This is Radicofani, that we nicknamed "The Radish." When touring this area and you are down on the roads in the valleys, disorientation can occur—especially for me if my wife is not along. Nothing Etruscan happened on Radicofani, but it is a great landmark and a wonderful one-hour side trip to the top and a climb into the partially restored castle.

Radicofani's claim to fame is that this isolated castle was the only safe stop on the Grand Tour for travelers on the leg of their journey from Siena to Rome. The view is panoramic and, when up there with bows and arrows and hot oil, the medieval owners felt safe, since no one could possibly assault the hill without being seen. Caution: the tower steps are narrow and shake a bit, so if you have acrophobia, as I do, hang on tight and inch your way around the rooms and parapets.

D. Mount Amiata

Finally, Monte Amiata will be discussed. At first blush, why bring into discussion Tuscany's highest point (1,400 meters or 5,702 feet), because no one would ever live this high up unless they were fleeing an enemy?

The drive to the peak is leisurely on switch-back roads. Enjoy the various views as you ascend; you will pass on the way to the summit several small villages that are perched on the side of the mountain. Just before the peak of the mountain (which is a narrow rock outcropping), a flat plateau appears. This area is used for parking and is surrounded by rustic cabins for rent by families who wish to hike and rest and vacation in the state park. Leave the car and walk to the top by a narrow trail and a few stone steps. The climb is steep, but even at my advanced age, no chest pain—Grazie Dio!

The distance is about four- to six-hundred yards, and in winter is used as a ski slope (surely one of the world's shortest slopes with a ski lift). At the top is a panoramic view of Tuscany. To the west, on a clear day, the coast is just visible, and to the east, we could see the hills, on one which our house was perched atop.

Telescopes are available for a few lira (now, a fraction of a euro) to look at the scenery and surrounding towns and farms. In the shadow of a military radar station are vendors selling an assortment of interesting artifacts. I bought my son (then age 14) a bottle of Che Beer (beer with Che Guevara's picture on the label for his college room in a few years). Why Monte Amiata? Well, adjacent to the parking area is a large open-air food market, so campers and hikers can stock up. Standing behind the tables of lumber balanced on carpenter horses are locals selling produce—some tailgating from the back of the trucks. All this is from their farms—and fresh.

Their faces look like the tomb paintings and sculptured figures on the sarcophagi and urns that we have seen so many of in the Etruscan sections of Italian museums. What they are selling is what I have been searching for lo these many years: a look, albeit brief, at the daily life of the Etruscan. I am surmising that the wheels of diverse cheeses, large coarse loaves of bread, cured hams, plump sausages, large dry salamis, smoked boar meat, green and black olives (dried and in brine), seasonal fruits, vegetables of all types, and hanging strings of garlics are exactly what the Etruscans of 2,500 years ago were ingesting. This includes the wonderful, full-bodied red wine they were selling, and in plain cork bottles—without the Madison-Avenue-produced art work on the labels of yuppie wine.

Here, finally, I found what I had been searching for these many years: an essentially unadulterated setting, unchanged for more than two millennia. No Roman, no medieval, no Renaissance patina to wash away; seeing the food that has sustained the peasant and his family for several millenia.

A final thought about the daily life of the Etruscan: every time I see blooming broom, I imagine the Iron Age huts of ancient Etruria relatively free of dust because of the endless supply of dried broom available for the compulsive Etruscan housekeeper!

11

Etruscans Outside Etruria

Before I close the cover on this search for the Etruscans, a few paragraphs seem appropriate to show where on the Italian peninsula Etruscans lived in close proximity to Tuscany, and where Etruscan material culture was traded about the known world in the ninth to third centuries B.C.

To begin, I will use contemporary Italian boundaries, so the reader can easily refer to any recent map. Ancient boundaries of these regions vary considerably, but the details of these changes are not important.

Let's start with northern Italy, in Liguria. Pisa is in the southern extremity, on the Arno River, and along the west coast of Italy as far north as Genoa was at times under Etruscan hegemony until about the fourth century B.C.

Umbria lies just adjacent to the east side of Tuscany, and the traveler looking for Etruscan sites constantly passes between the Tuscan and Umbrian borders. Orvieto lies in Umbria, and the Umbri, a separate people from the Etruscans, enjoyed close relations with them for centuries.

The province of Veneto has a long Etruscan history. The Po River as a southern boundary, and the Alps to the north, provided rich commercial activity dating back to the eighth and ninth centuries B.C. Adria, near the coast, on a branch of the Po River, was an Etruscan city and probably gave name to the Adriatic Sea. The province of Lazio contains Rome, on the Tiber River, its northern boundary, and to the south a string of ridges and hills which mark the end of the Appenine mountain chain extending into the Campania region.

This area, just south of Rome, is dotted with small pre-Roman cities, and Etruscan necropoli have produced treasures—many of them found in the Villa Gulia in Rome. (We have discussed Etruscan Rome at length in a previous chapter).

Just below Lazio, along the west coast, is Campania. This province is an archaeology park, for all practical purposes. To begin with, the earliest Greek city-states began in the western Mediterranean, in and around the Gulf of Naples. It is here the Etruscans found the Greek alphabet, which they adopted to their language—to this day indecipherable. Campania has possibly a southern extremity as the Gulf of Salerno. In the Gulf of Naples are found Cumae, Ischia, Capua, Pompeii, Herculaneum, Positano, Picentia—just to name a few sites that are familiar to many.

Throughout this entire region, the Etruscan footprint is found. South of Campania are the provinces of Lucania, Apulia, and Calabria, where Etruscan material culture has been excavated.

A few words seem appropriate about the islands of the western Mediterranean in the Tyrrhenian Sea. Corsica, Sardinia, and Elba are rich in metallic ores (iron, copper, lead, to name a few). The Etruscans produced an enormous amount of bronze statuary. The glass cabinets in every Etruscan museum are filled with one- to five-inch bronze pieces of every description of religious and secular life.

At the other end of the spectrum is the huge bronze Chimera found in Arezzo and discussed earlier in that section. This industry required huge amounts of raw ore for the furnaces, forges, and foundries on the mainland, and created the great wealth accumulated by Etruscan families. This afforded the monies necessary to purchase and import the Greek vases of unsurpassed beauty from Corinth and Athens, and to place them in their tombs to await delighted archaeologists 2,500 years later.

Surely their children kept a few on the mantle over the fireplace, just to enjoy or to hold the wine at the next Etruscan family wedding, bris, or christening.

Sicily, the triangular soccer ball that the tip of Italy keeps trying to boot, has produced Etruscan artifacts—even at the distant inland site of Mount Castellazzo di Poggioreale, in the Belici Valley at the edge of the plain of Marsala in western Sicily.

My very first dig was with Professor Albert Leonard Jr., at Mount Castellazzo, where a fragment of an Etruscan Bucchero kantharos (a table bowl with large ear-shaped handles) was found. Other areas where Etruscan material culture has come from the ground forms a great ellipsoid circle, beginning in Turkey to the east, then west through the Balkans, with heavy concentrations in central Europe, controlled by the Celtic tribes at that time. This includes modern Austria, Germany, Switzerland, and France. Etruscan goods followed the southern coast of France into Spain.

There was, of course, trade traced to the east: across the Adriatic Sea to the Dalmatian coast. The southern rim of this ellipse concludes the Carthaginian civilization in North Africa and then on to Egypt, Syria, and modern-day Israel and Lebanon.

As an aside, the longest Etruscan inscription ever found was written on linen wrapped around a mummy, found in Alexandria, Egypt. Unfortunately, it is an apparent religious calendar with not enough parts of speech and language structure to adequately decipher the Etruscan language. The Etruscan Rosetta Stone awaits unearthing. As mentioned earlier, someday, I predict, the key to unlock the language will be found along the shores of Lake Bolsena.

Cinerary Statue 4th c. B.C.

Terra Cotta Statue of Hermes 6th c. B.C. (Veio)

Bronze Helmet 5th c. B.C. with writing

Clay Geometric Jug 8th c. B.C. (Vulci)

Sarcophagus of Married Couple 6th c. B.C.

Bronze Mirror 4th c. B.C.

Marble Throne 1st c. B.C.

Bronze Cinerary Urn 8th c. B.C. (Bisenzio)

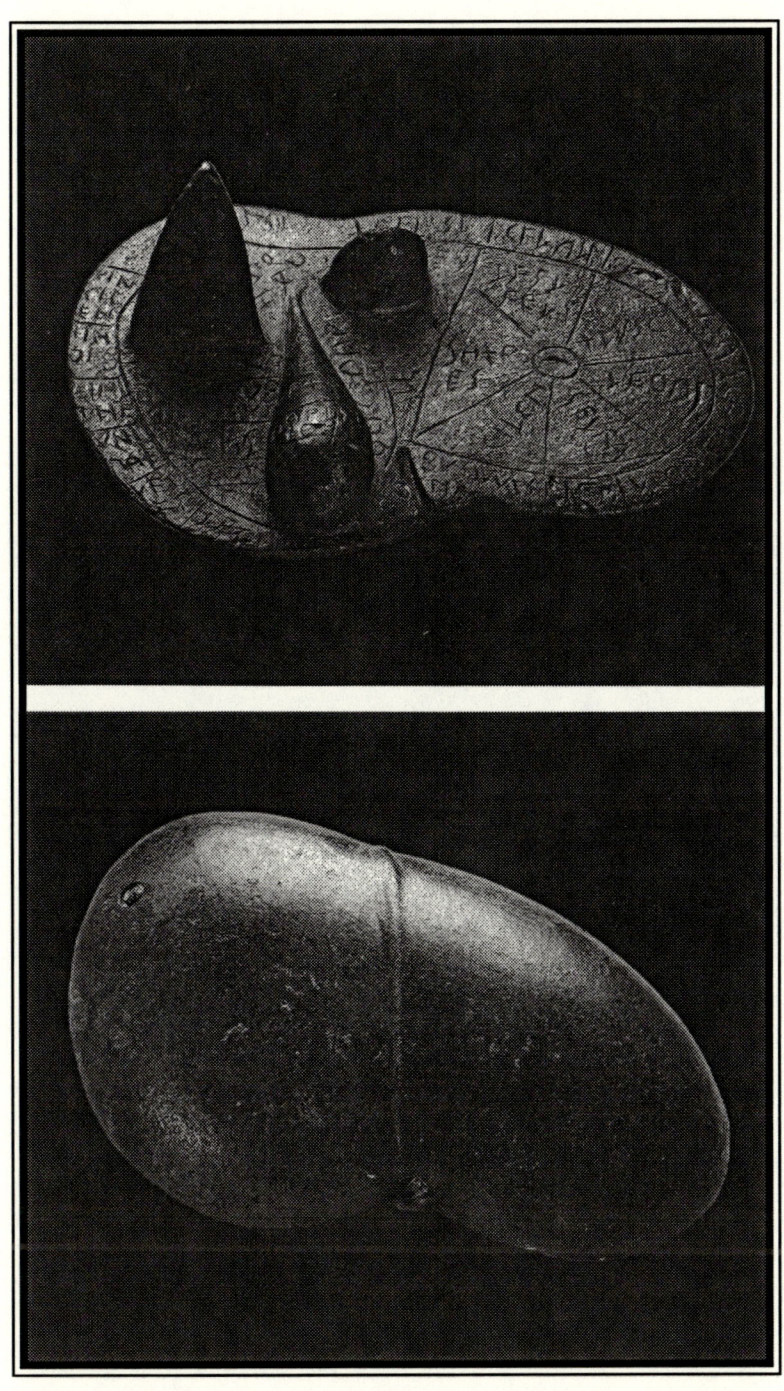

Bronze Sheep Liver used in Divination 1st c. B.C. (Piacenza)

Gold Fibula 6th c. B.C. (Vulci)

Bronze Chimera 5th c. B.C. (Arezzo)

Appendix

Major Etruscan Divinities
with Greek and Roman Equivalents

Etruscan	**Greek**	**Roman**
Aita (god of underworld)	Hades	Pluto
Apulu/Aplu	Apollon	Apollo
Aritimi/Artumes/ Aretume/Artemes	Artemis	Diana
Atunis	Adonis	*
Cel (mother goddess)	Ge	*
Culsans/Culsu (divinity of the gates)	*	Janus
Fufluns/Pacha	Dionysos	Bacchus
Hercle	Herakles	Hercules
Laran/Maris	Ares	Mars
Men(e)rva	Athena	Minerva
Nethuns	Poseidon	Neptune
Phersipnai	Persephone	Proserpina
Selvans (god of boundaries and fields)	*	Silvanus

Sethlans	Hephaistos	Vulcan
Suri (solar god with underworld aspect)	Apollo	Pater Soranus
Thesan	Eos	Aurora
Tin/Tinia/Tina	Zeus	Jupiter
Turan	Aphrodite	Venus
Turms (messenger god)	Hermes	Mercury
Uni	Hera	Juno
Vei	Demeter	Ceres
Veltha/Veltune/Voltumna (national god of Etruria and god of vegetation)	*	Vertumnus/Vortumnus

* no equivalent

(Modified from *Etruscan Civilization: A Cultural History* by Sybille Haynes)

Bibliography

This is a listing of some of the major publications I have used as resources to write this book. This includes travel books, guide books, journal publications, and historical monographs. These will give the reader a beginning, and will guide the traveler to several hundred other publications that are available on the history, the art, and the archaeology of the Etruscans.

Travel Books

D. H. Lawrence and Italy. 1998. Penguin Books.

Mark Twain. 1966. *The Innocents Abroad or The New Pilgrims' Progress.* Signet Classic.

Bill Bryson. 2001. *Notes from a Small Island.* Perenial–Harper Collins.

Ferenc Mate.1998. *The Hills of Tuscany: A New Life in an Old Land.* Delta.

Andrew Spender. 1992. *Within Tuscany: Reflections on a Time and Place.* Penguin Books.

Alain de Botton. 2002. *The Art of Travel.* Pantheon Books.

W. D. Howells. 1908. *Roman Holidays and Others.* Harper & Bros.

_____1867. *Italian Journeys.* Hurd & Houghton.

Katherine Hooker. 1918. *Byways in Southern Tuscany.* Charles Scribner's & Sons.

Journals

Etruscan Studies – Journal of the Etruscan Foundation, Vols. I–VIII, 1994–2001.

Morris M. Weiss, M.D. 1989. *Etruscan Medicine,* Journal of Paleopathology, vol. II, no. 3: pp. 129–64.

Guide Books
For Italy, Tuscany, and the Etruscans, I prefer the *Blue Guide Series*:
Rome and Environs
Tuscany
Northern Italy: From the Alps to Rome.
My second choice is the *Michelin Tourist Guides – Italy.*

Historical Monographs
Art, Architecture, Paintings and the History of the Etruscans.
George Dennis. 1878. *The Cities and Cemeteries of Etruria in Two Volumes.* John Murray.
C. Kerenyi: *Asklepios. Archetypal Image of the Physician's Existence*, translated from the German Bollingen Series, LXV 3. Princeton University Press, 1981.
Charles Godfrey Leland. 1963. *Etruscan Magic and Occult Remedies*, University Books.
R. M. Ogildie. 1976. *Early Rome and the Etruscans.* Harvester Press.
Massimo Pallottino. 1975. *The Etruscans.* Indiana University Press.
Emeline Hill Richardson. 1976. *The Etruscans: Their Art and Civilization.* University of Chicago Press.
Axel Boethius: *Etruscan and Early Roman Architectures,* Pelican History of Art, Penguin Books, 1978.
Otto J. Brendel. 1977. *Etruscan Art.* Pelican History of Art, Penguin Books.
Larissa Bonfante, ed. 1986. *Etruscan Life and Afterlife: A Handbook of Etruscan Studies.* Wayne State University Press.
Sybille Haynes. 2000. *Etruscan Civilization: A Cultural History.* The J. Paul Getty Museum.
Giovannangelo Camporeleale. 2004. *The Etruscans Outside Etruria.* The J. Paul Getty Museum.

Index

A

Abbazia di Monte Oliveto Maggiora 47
Abbazia di Speneto 3, 4, 6, 42
Adria 86
Aita 100
Alexandria – Egypt 88
Apulu 100
Arezzo 28, 51–53, 87
Aritimi 100
Arno River 2, 4, 8, 23, 26, 27, 33, 35, 51, 57, 65, 86
Atunis 100

B

Bagni della Serapi 18, 19
Belici Valley 88
Bologna 78

C

Campania 87
Capua 87
Casciano Thermae 23
Cel 100
Cerveteri 19, 58–60, 64
Cetona 55, 82, 83
Chianciano 18, 21, 22, 24, 25
Chuisi xiii, 8, 9, 10, 11, 21, 22, 56
Cloaca Maximus 76
Cortona 54
Culsans 100
Cumae 87

D

Dennis, George xiv, 104
Dionysius of Halicarnassus 2

E

Emperor Augustus 21, 22
Emperor Claudius 75
Emperor Flavius Honorius 32

Etruria v, 3, 5, 15, 16, 37, 54, 61–63, 65, 66, 68, 69, 85, 86, 101, 104
Etruscans xiii, xiv, xv, 1–5, 10, 15–18, 20, 24, 33, 35, 36, 40, 43, 48, 56, 57, 61–63, 65–67, 74–77, 83, 85–87, 103, 104
Etruscan Archaeology Museum – Siena 41
Etruscan Divinities 100
Etruscan Foundation 43, 103
Etruscan Studies – Journal 103

F

Fiesole 26, 28, 32–34, 66
Florence 4, 9, 10, 13, 15, 22, 23, 25–27, 29, 31–33, 39, 41, 51–53, 57, 65, 66, 69, 78
Fontes Clusini 18, 25
Fufluns 100

G

Grosetto 48–50
Guarnicci Museum – Volterra 37
Gulf of Naples 87
Gulf of Salerno 87

H

Hans Breitman 30, 31
Haynes, Sybille 63, 101, 104
Hercle 100
Herculaneum 87
Herodotus 1
Howells, William Dean xiv

I

Il Campo 39–42
Il Palio 39, 41, 42
Ischia 87
Italy xiv, xv, 2, 4, 6, 7, 9, 12, 15, 17, 21, 31, 32, 36, 39, 47, 48, 54, 57, 63, 82, 86, 87, 103, 104

L

Lake Bolsena 18, 19, 48, 67, 68, 69, 72, 88
Lake Trasimeno 54, 56
Laran 100
Lawrence, D. H. xiv, 103
Lazio 69, 86, 87
La Piana 3, 4, 42, 43, 45, 46
La Torre Ristorante 48
Leland, Charles Godfrey 15, 17, 29–31, 104
Leonard, Jr., Albert v, 60, 88
Leonardo da Vinci Airport – Rome 58
Liguria 86

M

Macadam, Alta 63
Maddelena 29, 32
Marcellus Burdigalensis 32
Men(e)rva 100
Mercato Nuovo 29
Montecatini 18, 22, 23
Montepulciano 11–13
Monte Amiata 84
Monte Oliveto Maggiora Monastery 47
Mount Castellazzo di Poggioreale 88
Murlo 45–47, 66
Museo Bandini – Fiesole 34
Museo Civico Archeologico – Chuisi 10
Museo Gregorian Etrusco – Vatican Museum 77

N

National Museum of Archaeology – Florence 10
Naukratis 60
Necropolis of Banditaccia – Cerveteri 58

O

Orvieto xiii, 59, 65, 67, 69–72, 86

Ottarino – Ristorante 28

P

Palatine Hill 77
Palazzo Vecchio 27
Piazza della Signoria 26–28
Pisa 12, 23, 35, 36, 41, 48, 51, 57, 65, 66, 86
Pompeii 87
Ponte Vecchio 26–28
Populonia 18, 65, 66
Positano 87
Prehistoric Museum – Monte Cetona 55
Pyrgi 60, 64

R

Radicofani 7, 83
Romans xv, 1, 3, 4, 10, 15, 16, 24, 33, 61, 62, 64, 71, 74, 75, 77
Roman Forum 40, 76
Rusellae 48, 49

S

San Casciano dei Bagini 24
San Gimignano 35, 66
Sarteano 41, 80–83
Saturnia 18–20
Sicily 7, 17, 57, 87, 88
Siena 3, 12, 23, 39–42, 44, 47, 57, 69, 83
Soren, David 21

T

Tarquin 61, 74
Tarquinia 19, 37, 58, 60–64, 73
Tempio di SanBiago 12–14
Temple of Aesklepios 75
Tenuto di Spannocchia 42
Thermae Montecatini 22
Tiber Island 75, 77
Tiber River 2, 4, 10, 73, 75, 76, 77, 86
Twain, Mark xiv, 103

Tyrrhenian Sea 2, 4, 57, 61, 73, 76, 87
Tyrrhenus 2

U

Umbria 11, 55, 70, 86

V

Vatican Museum 60, 77–79
Veneto 86
Vetulonia 48, 49, 64, 65
Villanovan 2, 33, 36, 54, 64, 78, 81
Villa Guilia 9, 10
Volsinii 69–72
Volterra xiii, 11, 18, 36, 37, 66

W

Whitehead, Jane 44, 45

About the Author

Dr. Morris Weiss is a practicing cardiologist. At the age of 40, he began working at classical dig sites around the Mediterranean Sea, toiling away as a laborer and doing study trips over the past 28 years.

The enigmatic Etruscan civilization became his obsession because of archaeology field experience and his studies in ancient medicine, with a concentration on Etruscan medical knowledge.

Printed in the United States
77140LV00007B/172-204